OPEN MINDS

OPEN MINDS

William F. Keefe

**The Forgotten
Side of
Communication**

**A Division of
American Management Associations**

Library of Congress Cataloging in Publication Data

Keefe, William Ford, 1921–
    Open minds.

    Includes bibliographical references.
    1. Communication in personnel management. 2. Psy-
chology, Industrial. I. Title.
HF5549.5.C6K373   658.3'14'0926   75-2412
ISBN 0-8144-5372-4

First Printing

To my parents, Walter and Marie

Preface

THE CRAFT OF MANAGEMENT is constantly receiving illumination, and necessarily. Growing sophistication among workers, coupled with an explosion of knowledge about man and his needs and drives, has produced challenges of Augean proportions. In response to demand, the quantity of guidance and instructional material has increased massively.

Too often such material ranges through obscure universes of ideation whose language is abstruse, whose dimensions cannot be specified, and whose practical significance remains in doubt. How to apply such material presents the manager with a problem: He simply cannot relate what he is reading to what he is doing on the job, whether in plant, office, shop, or laboratory. He cannot, on his own, marry the high-sounding principle to the concrete situation that faces him when he plants himself at his desk in the morning.

The case history that considers the specific principles behind the actual decisions provides the solution to the riddle. Here fact and problem can be wedded to abstraction, or guideline, or statement of policy. Beyond that, a story can be told in narrative form; the reader can see and feel with the subjects who faced the specific problem or problems, studied the possible alternatives, and acted. Pieces of communication that might have been used can be cited.

Such is the method of this book. Actual case histories, colorably changed, have been melded with many similar situations to become composites and therefore fictions that imitate life. In the end, it can be truly said: All persons, businesses, and situations shown in this book are entirely fictitious. Any resemblance to any person, living or dead, or to any existing or previously existing business is coincidental. My only purpose has been to illustrate certain concepts of communicating, of listening in particular. The imitation of life has extended even to names: Instead of using x or y to indicate people, I have chosen real-sounding names to add color and a sense of reality to the book.

My thanks to Carl Goodman, Helen Bugbee, and A.R. Finck for their valuable advice, aid, and suggestions on portions of the draft manuscript. Special thanks to Jerome C. Okonski for his constructive criticism.

WILLIAM F. KEEFE

Contents

Prologue

WHERE COMPLACENCY ONCE RULED, uneasiness has taken over. Students of employee motivation have come to recognize that a crisis was brewing even while they were rejoicing over the classic magnificence of recent work of the behavioral scientists. Suddenly it has become obvious that employee motivation cannot be approached impersonally or be treated as a technological problem. Men demand more. Solve one of their problems, meet one level of need that they share widely or universally, and another problem or need arises. The new challenge to the ingenuity of the motivator, or manager, may be greater than the one that preceded it.

The crux of the crisis does not lie in the theories that have been propounded—and applied with greater or lesser success. The crisis hinges on something else: on the spirit that informs the manager's approach to his people. He can be steeped in theory until it makes him self-conscious in his dealings with his peers, his subordinates, even his own children; he can make the requisite number of daily rounds of the plant; he can stay up nights studying the latest elaborations of concept. But not until he learns new ways of thinking and, in turn, new ways of *dealing* can he be really successful in negotiating the dark and nether region called motivation, a region where all kinds of devils of disorder and distrust are continually planting roadblocks and barriers.

At least one observer has put a blunt finger on the problem. "Most of the contemporary psychological conceptions of motivation take a reward-punishment psychology for granted," wrote Levinson. "They advocate trust and openness among employees and managers, but at the same time they acknowledge that the more powerful have a natural right to manipulate the less powerful."*

The assumption flowing from that gratuitous "acknowledgment"—that the powerful should, and by right do, have control over others, stands at the heart of the central problem of the seventies. For the assumption is both capstone and foundation stone—capstone of a Neanderthal philosophy of management and foundation stone of a welter of subordinate attitudes and opinions whose expression is not only inevitable but repetitive.

In short, either sooner or later, the manager will show his true colors. He cannot completely or forever mask his attitudes. If words do not give him away, his mannerisms and prejudices will.

Other flaws in today's approaches to management's need to motivate, and to motivate in such a way as not to *seem*, patently, to be motivating, have been isolated. Some theories that have been advanced as solutions for the problems of this plant or that plant, or of the whole kit and kaboodle of American industry, have been found to emphasize the wrong elements or dimensions of the management challenge. The developers of the theories may have the wrong motives, or they may be seeking to test concepts of which they are uncertain. (Few are more voluble in defense of their ideas than those who doubt the validity of those ideas.) And too often, the experience of the "experts" may lie in tech-

*Harry Levinson, "Asinine Attitudes Toward Motivation," *Harvard Business Review*, January-February 1973, p. 74.

nology rather than in management and organization theory and the psychology of behavior.

The current situation demands a new look at the whole series of theses and theories that govern management action. The new look, if it is to avoid the traps into which earlier theorists have fallen, must have its base in both theory and practice. The case history is an ideal way to show what can be accomplished in employee communication, in human relations, and, most essentially, in motivation as well as in theory itself. The manager must accept motivation as the name of the game. For what is the purpose of communication and human relations if not to motivate to optimal effort?

Similarly, theory must undergird practice or management behavior will deviate at times from the acceptable and truly practical. Worse, managers may worship false gods, obtain temporary results, and fail to see that they have been proceeding down dead ends. As one example, movement may be ascribed to motivation when it has really resulted from fear:

> To get people to do things as animals, you move them. When I respond as an animal because I want to avoid being hurt, that's movement. I called it KITA, for "kick in the a--." [But] when a human does something, he's motivated. The initiative comes from within.*

The ten case histories in this book have been adapted from actual situations to illustrate how some managers superinduced "initiative from within." Adaptations and adjustments have been introduced to clarify and simplify. In actuality, many of the cases were far more complex than they are presented here. That they echo the experiences of line

*"An Interview with Frederick Herzberg: Managers or Animal Trainers?" *Management Review*, July 1971, p. 5.

and supervisory foremen, middle managers, and others in the hierarchy of the typical industrial organization should not surprise; that they also suggest, in some cases, ranges of approaches to problems in communication and motivation should also be expected. In all likelihood, no theory that does not in practice leave room for individual ingenuity and creativity is worth a nickel. Nor, probably, has the manager thought through, or done justice to, the serious problems that confront him unless he has considered the entire range of solutions applicable under a given theory.

The question always is: How? One may grant that Theory Y is superior to Theory X, or that Theory Y_1 is superior to theories X, X_1, and Y. One may maintain that Likert's "systems" accurately reflect the most basic spectrum of choices open to the manager aware of the patterns in managerial and human behavior. But even then, one must make a choice of methods with which to implement theory.

The cases that follow indicate how ten managers went about making such choices. To some extent the dice are loaded against the manager or the foreman primarily involved in each case: Each situation carries an explicit, serious threat. But management itself is compounded of threats and challenges—if not today, then tomorrow. To be prepared for tomorrow, in the arena of communication and motivation, is to move *now* to solve the crisis of the seventies.

1

Mutiny on the Flagship

"Yes, I think a Hawthorne effect can be achieved in an entire workforce that is experiencing communications/morale bankruptcy. But whether it can be done without a major dramatic effort, such as the Hawthorne researchers employed and such as we used, is to be doubted."

— George R. Gallery, Plant Manager
RJB Corporation main plant
Calvin Park

MANAGEMENT-WORKER RELATIONS at the RJB Corporation's main plant at Calvin Park reached the zero level one morning in September 1969. It happened in the Little Conference Room. On the door hung a sign: "Grievance Meeting in Session." The door was closed, but the walls of the room were too thin to muffle the shouting inside.

Thursday, 10:30 A.M.

"This damn grievance shouldn't even be in the third stage! We should have settled it long ago!" —Mack Bergendorf, business agent of the International Association of Machinists and Aerospace Workers (IAM).

"What are we arguing for, then? All you guys have to do is be reasonable!" —Merv Hargit, director of industrial relations, RJB Corporation's Calvin Park plant.

"Be reasonable? This man has a real bitch, Merv! All over Fabricating foremen are doing the men's work." —Joe Allen, shop steward, Fabricating department.

"If you'd just listen, Merv, Joe's right. I told Grimm he wasn't supposed to be running more than 50 test pieces. But he ran and ran—he must've ran 200 of them." —Arthur Halvorsen, router operator, Fabricating department.

"You *told* him! Who in the merry hell said you could *tell* a foreman what to do?" —Merv again.

Outside, secretaries shook their heads. In the office of George R. Gallery (plant manager), next to the conference room, a worried Fred Tivanen, company vice president, operations, aired some complaints of his own.

Thursday, 10:40 A.M.

"This isn't the way you told me we were going to operate in the future, George. Where's the communications program Merv was going to start? Is that it in there? Where's the reduced flow of grievances? You've seen the grievance report—51 last month! That's a new record, more than we ever had before the strike."

George and Fred were still talking when the union men, jaws set, stalked out of the conference room, and slammed the door.

During the next week, five Fabricating department machines—routers, saws, and automatic screw machines—developed major problems that forced management to take them out of service.

FACEOFF AND FALLOUT

Gallery became impatient; in Fab's machine breakdowns he recognized the signs of near-mutiny, and the aftereffects of the faceoff in the Little Conference Room began to make themselves felt almost at once. Eventually they touched every one of the plant's 900 employees. George Gallery's management style changed. From the technical manager he had been, he started to become the complete manager; he paid attention not only to money, materials, and machines but also to men and motivation. He assessed the situation.

The problem was clear: Even the artificial, overformal upward communications technique embodied in the grievance procedure was breaking down.

1. You could look at it from an organization point of view: Is the organizational mode contributing substantially and heavily to the plant's problems?

2. You could examine and change the alignment of people within departments: Move managers to achieve a more specific, refined organization.

3. You could get down to the individual within the plant; see him as a person with needs, drives, ambitions, attitudes; and try to enable each person out there to change, to make the company's goals his own.

Negative on No. 1 and No. 2, Gallery decided. They amounted to piecemeal approaches. He had to reach the workforce in depth, become familiar with its problems, try to solve those problems and achieve better relations, better performance, an improved P&L statement.

Positive on No. 3.

Thursday, 4:30 P.M.

"What the hell went on in that conference room?" Gallery asked.

"George, I've been on this job for 23 years," Merv replied. "I know these people. You've got to pound your story into their thick skulls."

"There must be some other way. I want you to find it.

No—I want to find it with you. We're setting grievance records and we're going to find out why. Worst of all, we're missing the point. All these grievances are surfacing as expressions of unmet needs or unresolved problems. If we're getting hundreds of grievances, there are thousands of those problems and needs. Let's find out what they are."

Spotlight on the Behavioralists

If you were going for the jugular, seeking to influence the man at the machine, much of what the behavioral scientists had to say was pertinent.

Douglas McGregor said you make either Theory X or Theory Y assumptions. Under Theory X, you ride with the Mervs. Under Theory Y, you take an optimistic view of human behavior. Negative preconceptions go out the window. If given the chance, men will work without KITA. It could be so summed up.

A look at Abraham Maslow seemed wasted—at first. His "needs hierarchy" appeared too theoretical. His dictum, "a satisfied need no longer motivates," seemed simplistic.

But theories could not be studied discretely from the situation of the Calvin Park plant. Did this situation really answer its workers' needs to any substantial degree? To take Maslow's hierarchy from the bottom up . . .

1. Physiological
2. Safety need, including the emotional and physical factors
3. Need for belongingness and love, the first social need
4. Need for esteem
5. Need for self-actualization

. . . you would have to say no to the last three and probably no as well on No. 2. The tough, highly organized union took care of No. 1. It fought for job security, and seniority, and thereby protected the paycheck, which protected the dinner pail, and satisfied the physiological needs.

With Chris Argyris new clues appear. His effort to integrate the individual and the organization suggests a goal any manager should work toward. But do it through individuals in the organization who must first be trained and then thrown back into the Merv Hargit sea? The concept of laboratory training as a means of educating people to interpersonal competence is, admittedly, attractive. But what then? Expect that new competence to survive in this milieu? Expect it to stimulate better relations up and down the line? The whole plant should go to school at once—managers and workers alike.

Too much training goes down the drain. At best, training has long-range implications, not short-range. The same holds true for the theory of job teams or ad hoc work groups. Designing these would require reorganization, and to attempt reorganization in a plant with communications so constipated would invite broader chaos.

Rensis Likert is a new ball game. His ideas have direct and pressing meaning. The interaction-influence principle has two magnificent corollaries:

—The amount of influence a manager exerts over his subordinates is determined by how much he allows himself to be influenced by them, and

—The amount of influence a manager exerts upward and laterally determines the amount of influence he exerts downward.

And are we here not close to the solid, workaday finding that "the productivity and morale of employees improve to the extent that they are allowed to participate in the decisions that affect them on the job"?*

*Burleigh B. Gardner, and David G. Moore, *Human Relations in Industry* (Homewood, Ill: Richard D. Irwin, Inc., 1955, (Third Edition), p. 35.

But back to Likert. Assuming you like Theory Y, you would *have* to want to belong to the last of Likert's four "systems," his management style cosmology:

Exploitative-Authoritative
Benevolent-Authoritative
Consultative
Participative-Group

But *wanting* to belong never means you *do* belong. As manager you share the color and tone of those around you, including the Merv Hargits who front-run for you in so many hundreds of ways.

A riddle: Get rid of Merv Hargit? Replace him and others like him? Take over from them?

The Hawthorne parallel. Move on to behavioralist Frederick Herzberg—and farther. Your feet are planted firmly now. Herzberg's "motivation-hygiene" theory, keyed to the ways work and working conditions affect the lives of working people, point precisely where you want to go. Whether he identified the satisfiers (achievement, recognition, work itself, and so on) and dissatisfiers (company policy and administration, working conditions, supervision, and so on) with complete accuracy makes no difference; neither does the question whether they require more research for validation.

Neither, in fact, does the question whether they are called motivators and demotivators. They supply light, make sense. They suggest Hawthorne and F. J. Roethlisberger. Isn't the task at the Calvin Park plant exactly to reproduce the effects achieved by Mayo, Roethlisberger, and the Hawthorne researchers?

Can it be done in an entire plant? How?

Start with a dramatic break off from the current regime and thinking? Use a Hawthorne-style listening method?

Nothing else would do. No training could come close to meeting the need. No sensitivity training or organization development or group seminars or laboratory participation would help—all promised too little, too late.

Telling Whom—When

Gallery figured it out, noted down the protocol steps he would proceed through in introducing the program. He talked to James Byrne, the consultant who would conduct the in-depth listening program. Step by step Gallery began to clear the ground . . .

    A. Show and tell
        1. Top brass
        2. Merv
        3. Department managers
        4. Union leaders
    B. Kick off dramatically
        1. Foremen, department managers
           at Management Club
        2. Hourly personnel
           a. In writing
           b. Orally
    C. Follow through to give listener (ombudsman?)
       powerful direct and symbolic meaning
He encountered trouble only with Merv.

Wednesday

"You're going to spend all that dough on a consultant when we're just barely making it here?" Merv said.

"Right. I'll appreciate cooperation from your office, not only on the overall program but also on specifics like arranging meetings. The money? It'll be peanuts compared to what we're blowing on grievances in time lost, lawyers' fees, and all the rest."

The reaction of Marty Detterman, president of IAM Local

163, and the two union men who accompanied him was suprisingly agreeable, almost enthusiastic.

Thursday

"In short," Gallery said, "we need a completely new deal. We have to find a way to work together."

Detterman nodded. Then he asked questions: "Would a shop steward be allowed to sit in on the first meetings the consultant holds? Will plant management announce the program in advance? Will you give your word that the consultant will be allowed to remain independent? Would the grievance channels remain completely open? Are you [Gallery] taking over from Merv?"

Gallery evaded the last question, smiling; all the others he answered in the affirmative.

"We'll clear it with the boys," Detterman said. "Go ahead and set it up."

Diagnosis by ear. Even before the consultant began work, communications in the plant took on a new dimension. Three developments contributed to the changed atmosphere.

1. In accepting Gallery's suggestion that a listening consultant be brought in, top company management reached another decision of far-reaching import: Fabricating, the Calvin Park plant's largest department, would not be closed and moved away. Argument over the proposed move had raged for months, ever since the strike six months earlier. Fred Tivanen, from his aerie as vice president in charge of operations, said, "Close it." He believed that the department could compete and survive much better in a cheap-labor area. Gallery opposed him.

"No," Gallery said, "closing that department will have such repercussions throughout the rest of the plant that we might as well close all departments at once."

The grapevine had followed the controversy closely. Now the word flashed forth: Gallery, fighting for the integrity of the plant, had won out.

2. Gallery's stock rose meteorically among the rank and file. "The Man" had disagreed with a superior over an issue on which every man and woman in the plant could agree, and Fab would stay. When Tivanen resigned a few weeks later, it only spread frosting over a very satisfying cake.

3. Gallery announced the listening program skillfully. He followed, to some extent, the comments made by Consultant Byrne.

Monday

"Yes, we can produce a Hawthorne effect here," Byrne said. "But it has to start with you. We've got first to convince people that management is really serious in its pursuit of better relations as the key to higher productivity, more profit on sales, and so on. Then we've got to prove through action and communication that their conviction is based in reality. Then we're halfway home. People will look beyond their immediate situations and problems to management's good intentions and management's interest."

"How long could this take?" Gallery asked.

"No way to tell. It can be fast or slow," Byrne answered. "You'll want to make a deliberate effort to throw off all baggage—the reservations and prejudices, the knee-jerk reactions. These inevitably grow on a man in this type of situation. Look at Merv. Then you'll want to work to get as much cooperation as possible out of your management staff, down to foremen. Don't be too nice a guy about it; we're fighting for money: profit. Tell them their jobs are at stake—politely. If you also tell them you're trying to get people working up to their full potential, you'll bring the good ones along."

Gallery called a special meeting of the Management Club to announce the new effort. The meeting took place on a Friday night. Gallery made his key points in a talk that Byrne helped him prepare (see Exhibit 1-1). "We are looking for a whole new way of life here," Gallery said, "one that will be easier for all of us."

The following Monday morning the announcement of the program appeared on all the plant bulletin boards (see Exhibit 1-2). The announcement was low key, simple. It answered as many employee questions in a short space as could be foreseen in advance. The consultant would start work in nine days, and personnel participating in the informal conference sessions with him were asked to feel free to communicate their suggestions, complaints, ideas.

That afternoon Gallery met with his department managers. He asked them to watch for reactions to the listening program. A couple of them had heard comments already—Blanchard in Fabricating and Ventura in Shipping/Receiving. The comments ran to nuts and bolts: "What made the company decide on this?" "Can we get some of these safety problems cleared up?" "It's about time they did something like this."

The department managers had begun to listen. Diagnosis by ear had begun even before the consultant started.

The first day. Byrne went to work at 8 A.M. From time to time during that first Wednesday, Gallery heard reports of his progress. In sum, they indicated all was progressing well. Workers were not only attending the meetings on a voluntary basis, they were asking if others in their departments would be allowed to take part later.

A foreman balked. He had been notified that four of his subordinates were to be released at a specified time to attend a conference, but when the time came he discovered an "emergency" and kept the men on the job. "Where are they?" asked his department manager, Ventura.

1-1 Highlights of George Gallery's Kickoff Speech Before the Management Club.

Good evening.

It seems that every time I come to a Management Club meeting I'm asking for something. This time is no exception. I'm asking for your cooperation.

We've been looking for a solution to a lot of problems. The biggest of these seems to be our communications problem. That in turn has given us a morale problem of monumental proportions.

Now we think we have an approach. Starting in two weeks, a listening consultant will be visiting our plant one day a week. He'll be talking to workers in all departments, getting their ideas. He'll be talking to foremen — area foremen, general foremen, department managers — getting your ideas.

Every single idea that we receive will be studied. Wherever we can, we will take action. I realize that we'll hear gripes, complaints, bitches, a little of everything. We are going to listen to every single one. We are going to study every single one to find out what we can do to improve our plant and its operations.

We're looking for a whole new way of life here, one that will be easier for you, me, our employees— all of us.

1-1 (Cont.)

By starting a dialogue throughout the plant we think we can do it, if everyone pitches in.

I don't have to tell you what our long-range goals are. But I will.

— We want to make open, free communication the stepping-stone to better, smoother, more cooperative team effort.

— We want to seek out and find those employee problems that blossom into grievances — find them and solve them in advance.

— We want to get every single employee on the company's bandwagon, encourage everyone to think company rather than thinking problem, argument, sabotage.

— We are going for broke — trying to reverse the poor morale trend we've suffered along with for years.

— We're trying to put this plant on its feet, to make some money. If we do it, we'll all benefit.

We've got to stop shouting at one another; we've got to listen to one another, really listen.

Some of you will say, "They're going around the foremen, jumping levels of command, checking on us." Don't believe it for a second. We couldn't care less about that aspect of this program.

1-1 (Cont.)

But do believe this: We have a job to do here and it's not getting done. We're now asking — demanding — that it get done.

We want, and must have, cooperation and the ideas, the creative thinking of every employee — you included.

Our survival may depend on whether, by making everyone a living part of this organization, we can get cooperation from our people. Your roles, your status remain basically unchanged. You still have the demanding full-time challenge of your jobs, and believe me, I know those jobs have gotten harder over the years.

Let's make them easier. Let's see if we can solve some people problems.

We want productivity. More innovation. Better use of our physical and human resources. We want open minds, creativity. We want profitability, supervisory responsibility. Performance. The best that every worker has in him.

Join with me in this campaign to turn this plant around. Believe me, all our futures — our jobs — depend on how well we do.

Thank you.

1-2. Bulletin board announcement of the listening program.

TO ALL EMPLOYEES:

Good communications can help make our company successful. Employees' ideas can make it possible for us to become the best plant in our industry.

To put these ideas to work we are starting a new program. James Byrne, a consultant on business communications, will visit our plant weekly starting Wednesday, November 11. He will talk with management personnel, including foremen, and with groups of hourly workers. He will have several goals while working with our Calvin Park plant:

— To learn about our products and how we do things in both the management and production areas.

— To gather ideas that will help us improve our position in our industry and our community, our operations, and our planning.

— To make recommendations on how we can improve communications and build teamwork at all levels.

1-2 (Cont.)

Comments from a number of employees have indicated that such a program will be of value. I can promise you that we will give full consideration to every suggestion given to Mr. Byrne or turned in to us through foremen.

We hope in starting this program that we can prepare for future growth. We are entering a period in which we will be facing many new challenges. It is important to each of us that we do everything possible to keep abreast of or beat our competition.

I feel sure all of you will cooperate fully in this effort to keep our plant moving forward.

George R. Gallery
Plant Manager

Wednesday, 2:45 P.M.

"Are you serious about this thing?" the foreman asked.

"Certainly am," Ventura said. "Those men are 15 minutes late now. Get them to that conference table in the library and do it fast. This is George's program and we're not going to foul it up."

The foreman tried again. "We've got all this stuff to get out by 3:30—"

"You knew yesterday that these men were to have this time off. You had all their names. You should have planned it better. Now get them to the meeting."

Gallery met Byrne at the end of the day. The consultant came into the office area looking tired. It was 6 P.M. and Merv had left; he never stayed overtime.

Wednesday, 6 P.M.

"How'd it go?" Gallery asked.

"What a massive outpouring." Byrne showed a ruled pad filled with notes. "I've never seen anything like it. Some of those people said they had never had a chance to talk to anyone before."

"It could be true," Gallery said. "Where do we go from here?"

"Hold fast," Byrne suggested. "Keep stressing that you want cooperation at all levels. Keep a tight rein on your IR department, it's held in very low esteem. Don't hesitate to get out on the floor yourself and talk to people. And one more thing: can you have someone break down the grievances you've had in the past six months, by type or section of the contract? I want to see if there's a correlation between the grievances and my notes."

The survey was taken. The correlation between the grievances and Byrne's notes was close, but the comments in the notes covered a far broader range, from policy to the working atmosphere of the plant, on to supervisory techniques and to nitty-gritty workplace problems.

Gallery insisted that department managers and foremen take action on the latter wherever possible. "Exceed your budget temporarily if you have to," he said over and over again.

Action came. An overhead hoist was said to be a safety hazard. A maintenance foreman checked it and confirmed that a wheel could leave its track at one point. A work order was issued and the hoist was repaired. Holes in the floor in Fabricating made it difficult for materials handlers to move raw materials carts. The holes were filled in. Broken windows allowed cold air to flow into a breakroom in Shipping/ Receiving. The windows were replaced.

One thing became clear: In offering a forum for discussing gripes, complaints, constructive suggestions, creative ideas, management had suggested to workers that relief would be forthcoming where possible. Where it was impossible, reasons would be given by Byrne or others: too costly at this time, or impracticable for technical reasons, or conflicts with plans for change already in the works. Gallery made certain that the answers going back to workers through Byrne were both cogent and truthful. Gallery was building trust.

TALK TO THE GUY

Talk to the guy—this, in oversimplified form, was Byrne's formula. But he expanded on that. He gave Gallery a list of the communications goals they would work toward to spread the gospel of listening:

□ Make genuine listening the cornerstone of all managerial communications.

□ Find out in workers' own words what their feelings and attitudes and ideas are.

□ Use this information to guide management policies and programs, in both the operational and the communications spheres.

□ Help managers to become more aware of problems and trends and to be prepared for change so they can prepare their own people for change.

□ Encourage workers to listen to management on the theory that "good listening begets good listeners."

□ Open all channels of communication—upward and downward—in a systematic, sensitively attuned, objective, action-oriented way.

□ Use all available means of communication to supplement listening.

□ Open up minds—workers' and managers'—by showing in practice that listening has the unique power to reduce the dimensions of problems: Having spoken to someone who really listens, a worker has the feeling that he has already accomplished something.

□ Work fast; the forces aligned against you have had years to grow.

Background of Strife

The history of conflict could be charted without difficulty. Some 20 years earlier, when the plant had been employing about 500 workers, employees had voted in the IAM. Management had recoiled, expressing its feelings succinctly: "If that's what they want, that's what they'll have—and nothing else." The annual picnic fell by the wayside. A gulf developed between workers and management.

Employees had cast a majority of yes votes for what they felt were good reasons. For one thing, employees wanted more job security and more fully developed and carefully observed personnel and labor relations policies. In particular they wanted firm adherence to a seniority program that recognized longevity primarily in layoff, recall, and similar situations.

Even with the union in, many employees still felt strong loyalty toward their family-owned company. But in the new dispensation these loyalties were largely snubbed. Management decided to look upon all its workers as union members, as employees who had betrayed the company and must be held accountable for their mistake.

Strike and strike again. Four years after the union election the plant experienced its first strike. Afterward, strikes occurred at least every four years—and in one six-year stretch they occurred at the conclusion of each two-year contract.

Some of the strikes produced violence that made local headlines. The plant became notorious. Merchants in Calvin Park and nearby Frankfort reduced their inventories when contract negotiations were coming to a climax; they knew that if a strike took place, buying power in the community would automatically drop off.

The merchants also took direct action. Twice they sent delegations to the plant's top management and to the union to plead for forbearance—to no avail. They received short shrift from both sides.

Gallery was the plant's first truly professional manager. He had been on the job for only a year when the next strike began. He was brought up short. He had felt he was making headway with a new policy that called for more union-management discussion, more cooperation. As a symbol of his goodwill, he had formed a Problem-Solving Committee including membership from both the union and the management sides.

The committee had met twice when contract negotiations began. At that point the committee died. "A distraction at this time," the union men said. In effect, they wanted no negotiating outside their own meetings with the management team.

The strike tested Gallery's professional convictions to the core. He felt a strong temptation to take a more combative stance toward the union and its militant leadership. But he fought the temptation, and after the strike he called the union's leaders into his office. Merv was present but not actively participating.

Monday

"We'd like to close ranks and try to establish a better atmosphere around here," Gallery said.

The union men were skeptical. "We believe you want a better atmosphere, Mr. Gallery," Marty Detterman said. "We want the same. After all, our people work here—no work, no paycheck, no bread and butter. But we don't think a lot of people around here share your feelings." He didn't look at Merv.

Problem isolation, goal development. Byrne and Gallery worked against that background. They placed the statements of management people alongside the comments of workers to piece together group attitudes. The plant's root problems seemed to be five:

1. Intransigence on management's side initially, stemming from the plant's unionization.

2. Development in many middle managers and foremen over the years of a "combat psychology" that perpetuated the high-level obduracy.

3. Progressive loss of interest on the part of management in communications and other policies and programs that could possibly have improved the situation.

4. Lack of strong leadership that could demand and effect a reversal of the trend.

5. Over time, total loss of worker trust and confidence in management and its motives and loss of willingness in many foremen to take even normal responsibilities.

From study of the consultant's notes and all other available data, including grievance reports and statistics, a single major conclusion was reached: As originally foreseen by Gallery, the work of removing or reducing demotivators or irritants should go on. At the same time other programs would be undertaken to open up the entire communications climate of the plant. Hopefully, the result would be improved morale first and a higher level of work motivation second.

A blueprint for the future evolved as management—Gallery—made the decisions logically flowing from his initial assessments.

Management had to set its sights on developing a healthy human relations climate. That choice made, it had to live and breathe human relations. The various members of management had to become human relations-conscious and human relations skillful: people-centered without being paternalistic or overly permissive.

Economics and financial considerations could not be allowed to unnecessarily impede physical improvement, the removal of demotivators, the establishment of an effective communications program. A judgment factor became all-important: Top management had to participate directly to push selected initial projects that appeared necessary even where they "cost too much." Admittedly, the lack of a human relations climate could not be corrected with money alone. But money suddenly had importance because workers looked for action on the work floor. Past neglect of even the rudiments of a human relations policy had become costly.

Concomitantly, or perhaps initially, management had to make some assumptions about work and workers. Management had to clarify its own positions to itself. Did workers take to work naturally? Did they basically want to work? Would they work if given the appropriate environment? If it had once existed, could that fundamental characteristic survive without nourishment over the years, or could years of tension and disagreement eradicate it as a moving force? A gamble was involved here. The Calvin Park plant's workers might generally have lost the basic drives to work and to take pride in accomplishment on the job.

"We are taking the risk," Gallery decided. "We believe they want to work."

The formal organization might have to be restructured later, but initially management saw it as incidental, not as the controlling influence in the plant's situation. In any circumstances, management reasoned, the organizational format existed mainly on paper, a fact that would be true in most companies. In the Calvin Park plant, lines of influence, control, communication, and authority ran in all directions, up, down, and laterally. Everyone knew it and accepted it. Also, the formal organization had survived in times of both good and poor morale. The form of organization had to be regarded as secondary.

An entirely new philosophy of discipline had to be evolved. Management in the person of George Gallery consciously decided that in "punishing" workers and the union it was often spitting in its own soup. The whole thesis on which family or family-appointed managers of the past had operated was cast aside; no longer could management afford to view as punishment its rejection of union overtures, its deliberately poor communications track record, its intransigence in negotiations and grievance sessions, its support of hard-nosed foremen. None of those approaches could now be regarded as any more than immature expressions of either incompetence or pique, neither of which could play a role in a professionally managed firm. None of those approaches, in fact, had ever produced anything more than worker retaliation.

Discipline, of course, still had to play a role in the plant's operations. The punitive provisions of the contract and its codicils had to be carried out or charges of favoritism could justifiably be leveled. For example, where a union-management agreement specified that a worker would receive a warning after three or more unexcused absences in a two-month period, that warning would be issued. But punishment is administered with varying degrees of harshness. If administered without recrimination, gently, its imposition leaves lighter scars.

Facing the unavoidable. Inevitably, management had to face up to one other question: Could it reestablish its overall objectives and set general policies that would lead it toward achievement of those objectives?

Here, decision proved more difficult. A fundamental change of policy based on revised approaches in key areas would in all likelihood lead to changes of key personnel. Merv, for example, might have to go eventually, perhaps when his policies had been shown to be totally bankrupt. The jobs of some department managers and foremen might also be on the line.

Beyond that, basic changes in objectives and policies entailed risks. Uncertainty and its companion, insecurity, might result. The policy that Merv represented was at least a known quantity.

Gallery ran the risks. The evidence Byrne was gathering from workers contributed mightily to the decision.

Wednesday, 10:50 A.M.

"This is a safety problem," the union steward said, "and it's been kicking around in grievance channels for years. But maybe you can do something about it."

"I can't really go around the grievance procedure," Byrne

said. "But I can ask about anything."

"Why don't you ask about this? Our guys in dipping are working with epoxy paints. But here's a newspaper article that says these paints are hazardous to health. Now with this new action program, maybe management will at least check it out. We're getting a lot of other things done, maybe we can get action on this too."

Wednesday, 4:45 P.M.

"Who's running this plant anyway," the man from Cordonite said. "Gallery's okay, but he's got to kick some tails."

"What do you mean?" Byrne asked

"You know. He's got to run the place. Tell people like Hargit and his crew what they're supposed to do. Set the policy for them and then ride them to make sure they carry it out."

"Operation open mind." So the consensus surfaced. Workers were weary of tension, argument, strife. Strong management leadership was needed to accomplish valid goals. Workers saw hope of relief in the new direction represented by Byrne and sponsored by Gallery.

Management responded. In consultation with his department managers Gallery settled on a simple set of human relations policy objectives (Exhibit 1-3). To make sure they penetrated all management ranks, he incorporated them into a new Foreman's Policy Manual. Over Merv's objections he ordered the manual prepared in loose-leaf form and inscribed with the company name and the name of each individual in line management. It was to be issued even though it was still in the formative stages; policies would be added as time went on. Eventually, all basic areas of interest and responsibility, including discipline and communications, would be covered.

1-3 Basic human relations, policy guidelines.

Good human relations makes for smooth operations. People can work together without friction. Costly disagreement and irritation are reduced to a minimum. The work proceeds safely and effectively and without confusion or waste. Neatness, cleanliness, and orderliness—good housekeeping—become easier. Employees have confidence in superiors and respect for them; employees can enjoy their work.

The following simple, streamlined guidelines are suggested as the key ways to achieve good human relations:

— Foster the greatest possible degree of participation by subordinates in decision making.
— Encourage a free flow of both ideas and criticism.
— Treat every subordinate as an individual with individual capacities, needs, skills, and ambitions.
— Announce changes in advance where possible and always explain changes in detail as soon as possible.
— Show interest in and respect for every employee so as to make each one feel part of our team.
— Recognize and give credit to subordinates who turn in good ideas or excel in performance.
— Lead by communication and persuasion rather than by driving through fear; tell why and ask for cooperation.
— Be firm, fair, and consistent in administering discipline, and always reprimand privately.
— Stress help, training, and encouragement for subordinates as ways to enable them to learn and, if possible, to advance.
— Maintain integrity in all dealings with subordinates.
— Give subordinates the benefit of the doubt wherever doubt exists.
— Make listening the cornerstone of your individual communications approach; never be too busy to listen.

Gallery's introduction to the manual is shown in Exhibit 1-4.

The start had been made. "Operation Open Mind" was launched. Gallery saw the introduction of the policy manual as the official beginning of his effort to reach his management team with an entirely new way of thought. To mark the event he made a formal presentation of the manuals to the first group of foremen.

Monday

"We are depending on you men," he told the foremen. "It will be you who can make this program succeed—you who can, if you want, make it fail. We are counting on you to throw your weight behind it. We are calling it Operation Open Mind. In starting it formally today, we are asking that you take a new look at the whole set of relationships in your areas to see how they can be improved, that you review every single problem you face to see if you, or we and you, can solve it, that you give us your ideas on how your experience can be generalized to solve problems throughout the plant."

Gallery had already sketched out the next steps he wanted to take to realize Byrne's recommended ways to spread the listening gospel:

□ Starting with the policy manual, launch new internal communications formats to make the task of reaching the worker both practicable and easy. Use these new devices to (1) make it clear to workers that the plant's management, up and down the line, intended to work for better relations; (2) clarify for all workers the "state of the plant" so that they would know the importance of their roles and what was at stake in the future; (3) guide management down to line foremen in ways that could help push the program forward.

□ Close the broad social gap between management and worker.

1-4. Introduction to Foreman's Policy Manual.

No company, no business can progress today unless it has high-quality management personnel. Managers and supervisors are the sergeants, lieutenants, and captains who make an operation go. Their efforts are essential to the success of every major company program. On the most basic level, they represent the company to employees and employees to higher management.

The purpose of this manual is to provide a better understanding of our plant's policies, programs, and procedures: how and why we work as we do. With such understanding the management task of each of us will become simpler.

Supervisors, in particular our foremen, are our front-line personnel officers. They deal with the problems and challenges of the workplace on an hour-by-hour, day-to-day basis. They must be able to obtain the cooperation of employees both in getting the work out and in putting our programs and policies into effect. They can best use the guidance that a Foreman's Policy Manual provides; to them, our foremen, this Manual is dedicated.

We are also dedicating this Manual to the theme of universal cooperation and teamwork throughout our plant. We believe that, properly used, this Manual will:

- Make the foreman's job easier by letting him know what is expected of him.
- Prevent misunderstandings.
- Make it possible for Calvin Park plant supervisors, managers, and staff departments to reach similar decisions in similar situations in different parts of the plant.
- Help guarantee fair and considerate treatment of all employees.

This Manual is not complete and never will be. It is designed for continuous growth. Portions will be added as they are needed; other portions will be replaced from time to time. Nothing is so final that it cannot be succeeded by something better; we will

1-4 (Cont.)

remain flexible. The ideas of managers and supervisors will be welcome as the process of growth goes forward. While our union contract spells out specifics of our union—management relationship, this Manual will develop broad policy goals and provide guidance material where none exists.

No collection of rules or policies can ever replace good judgment. Rules and policies can only guide judgment and method. Nor can any set of policy statements ever be all-inclusive. They can never give ironclad answers to every work problem, or take the place of reasoned responses. In a word: Employees' questions should never be disposed of with the statement, "It's company policy." On the contrary, the reasons for a policy provide the material for such answers. Wherever possible, this Manual will give reasons why a policy has been established.

We want the questions and suggestions of every foreman and manager so that we can make this Manual a living and useful reference guide for all.

George R. Gallery
Plant Manager

◻ Gradually expand communications efforts into media outside the plant—newspaper, radio, and others.

◻ Train foremen in human relations and communications.

◻ Set up formal means by which management personnel could contribute ideas to help move the program ahead, including a Foreman's Steering Committee to formalize this portion of the program in ways the foremen themselves would suggest and idea blanks, which would be available to all foremen to use to submit ideas. One copy of each blank submitted would go into the individual foreman's personnel folder, to be taken into consideration when six-month performance reviews were made out.

DISTORTION'S UGLY HEAD

Wednesday

Where people are concerned nothing proceeds in a straight line.

"The men are six feet high about one thing," Joe Allen said, "and that's this FA business."

"Never heard of it," Byrne said.

"We just heard about it ourselves. The men are calling it 'Fat A--.' The problem is that they've put numbers on every machine in Fab. Our guys think management is working up to a quota system—you know, so many pieces an hour. Some foremen have already started chewing guys out for not making the quota."

"No one explained what it was?"

"Not really."

The truth of FA, as Byrne heard it from Gallery, was far from dire. Fab management, represented by the industrial engineering staff, had posted the numbers to launch a Fault Assessment program. The program had legitimate cost control aims: to keep tabs on the work input on every order, to ascertain which jobs were money makers and which were losers, and eventually to enable management to drop those orders that were not making money or find a way to make them profitable.

A brief notice written by the IE department had been posted. No one read beyond the "cost efficiency" phrase in the first sentence—and the notice disappeared from the Fab bulletin boards in a couple of days. The following Monday, day-shift operators reaching their routers, punch presses, drills, and other equipment found the "quota" numbers posted. The numbers actually represented an educated guess concerning each machine's per-hour productive capacity on various types of orders.

A valid purpose: to learn which jobs were profitable and which were not. But a storm was brewing in Fab. One worker had almost come to blows with his foreman. The worker's machine had not performed up to target capacity and the foreman had chewed him out.

Wednesday

"I'd suggest some fast action," Byrne said. "Every Fab group complained about this today."

"I knew they were going into this program," Gallery said. "I approved it. But all I've heard since Monday is that it is working well."

"A classic case of distortion," Byrne shot back. "The workers took the whole cost efficiency approach as an IE trick to impose a quota system. Some foremen are using it as a club to pound more work out of their people. You're getting nothing but favorable reports when Fab is on the verge of revolt. The good news filters up. The bad news is eliminated."

"Where do we go?"

"First, verify what I'm telling you. Second, you want

new communication devices. How about a very simple, one-sheet bulletin that you could grind out in an hour or two to issue spot news items of all kinds?"

"Can do. We could mimeograph it."

"Next, have Blanchard talk personally to every man in Fab, in groups, to explain FA. And ask Blanchard to tell all his foremen that FA is not to be used as a disciplinary tool in any way, shape, or form."

Gallery and Blanchard followed through. Tempers cooled. The first issue of the *Spotnews* had been devoted primarily to an article on FA (Exhibit 1-5). Blanchard met with all his workers and foremen and told union officials *and* foremen that the FA target figures could not be used for disciplinary purposes.

The *Spotnews* began to appear two or three times a month. It was read eagerly.

Distortion plus. Workers began to cooperate in the FA program. Day by day reports came in from the Fab floor: The FA target on router 210 was too high; the target on mill 458 was too low; a minor machine adjustment on punch press 23 would make it possible to meet the machine's target. A method of gauging cost had become a motivational tool. Productivity began to climb.

Gallery became aware of the frequent distortion in upward communication. He found other disturbing examples:

The story: "Several" CO_2 fire extinguishers had been installed in Cordonite where fires might start in electrical equipment. *The fact:* One CO_2 extinguisher had been installed.

The story: Weeks ago the vending company servicing the plant had promised to keep the vending machines at sites 3 and 6 in Maintenance and Shipping/Receiving filled for second-shift personnel. *The fact:* The vending machines still ran out of food in midafternoon, on schedule.

1-5. Spotnews article on the Fault Assessment Program.

FAULT ASSESSMENT PROGRAM
LAUNCHED IN FABRICATING

"Keep the orders coming!" That's the motto of the Fault Assessment program—FA—that has been launched in our Fabricating Department.

Created by Fab's Industrial Engineering Department, the program has the main purpose of telling management which jobs coming to Fab are profit makers and which are profit losers.

"What this program amounts to is that, for the first time in the history of Fab, we have a tool that we can use to gauge the amount of work going into every Fab order," said John Blanchard, Fab department manager. "Work input is our biggest cost factor.

"With FA we will be able to eliminate some jobs that are actually losing us money. More important, with attention to the details of this program, with some machine changes and other improvements we'll be able to keep all of our current customers. We even hope to pinpoint some machine problems that Engineering can solve.

"If we can do that, we'll be able to bid on jobs for which we could never compete before. That would mean more orders for Fab, more work for our manufacturing departments—and, we hope, more jobs in our plant."

Launched last Monday, FA involves setting a "production target" for every machine and every type of job. The targets are posted on the machines to tell operators how many parts each machine is expected to produce. Meeting a target means, generally, that a reasonable profit margin is being achieved.

"Operators' comments and help in making the targets as realistic as possible will be welcomed." Blanchard stressed that such comments and ideas "will be essential to the success of the program" and should be turned in to foremen.

1-5 (Cont.)

"We should also stress that our target figures are only educated guesses," Blanchard continued. "We are taking the optimum production speeds given us by the manufacturers of our equipment, figuring in the machines' ages and physical condition, estimating our labor costs, and taking other factors into consideration.

"Our FA targets will remain in force for two months. A review of all the targets will then be conducted and adjustments made. The adjustments will be made primarily on the basis of operators' ideas and suggestions and the records of each individual machine.

"We are a big job shop. We work with a lot of different materials—sheets, laminates, and so on. We fill about 20,000 orders a year. We know we've been losing money on some of these orders and that just isn't healthy.

"We're hoping FA is the answer."

The story: The problem of fumes from the propane gas trucks was being solved. A number of different filters were being tested. *The fact:* One truck had a filter, and it worked. Nothing else had been done about the problem.

Gallery decided that the matter was serious enough to discuss with his department managers.

Monday

"Please watch for this," Gallery said. "We're finding a lack of follow-through. We're getting reports that things are happening when they aren't. We're getting fact distortion. This happens in all plants to some extent. You get selective reports coming up the line. The foremen and area foremen aren't entirely to blame; everyone has a tendency to pass on the good news and filter out the bad. But this can hurt us.

"I'd like you to be careful about this. There are four or five things to watch for. One, make sure you're not hearing only—or mostly—about the things in which you're interested. Two, make sure you're getting the *whole* story when you get any story. Three, make sure we're not losing things in channels. If we promise hourly people that something will be done, and it's not done, we're in trouble. Four, watch for the quick answer. We've gotten a lot of them recently and some have proved to be wrong. Five, if you see a way—short of changing our organization around—of shortening the lines of communication, or making them more direct, let's look at it. We may get into changed organization later—decentralize and hopefully make communicating faster and more accurate."

Once burned, forever learned. A fire proved that Gallery had communications distortion within his own IR department.

One Sunday in January a skeleton crew was on duty in the

tower area, a five-story appendage to the main plant that was largely used for warehousing and raw materials sorting operations. The fire, beginning in rags in a corner of the sorting area, spread to the second floor. Two hours later, when the blaze had finally been extinguished by the plant's own fire fighters and the Calvin Park fire department, $30,000 worth of damage had been done.

Gallery received a report from Merv Hargit's safety engineer, Mal Gowron: All hands had performed well; all fire-fighting equipment had been accessible and in top shape; the fire fighters had arrived in minutes; the fire had been "one of those things."

Byrne talked to some men who worked in the tower. His notes turned up a number of comments on factors that had contributed to the loss (see Exhibit 1-6). Investigating, Gallery found most of the comments were accurate. He went back to Merv and Gowron.

Friday

"Some of these things should have been taken care of," Gallery said.

"George, you know we're working on a shoestring," Merv said. "We can't get OKs to buy these minor items—ever."

"You can now. See me next time you want to buy new equipment. But some of these comments have nothing to do with buying. Let's make sure we get straight facts on safety problems."

Hawthorne effect stymied. On the positive side, Gallery received more evidence that a Hawthorne effect was developing. Byrne had been on the job three months.

In Fab, a new type of exhaust vent was being installed on machines where dust appeared to be a problem.

1-6. Excerpts from James Byrne's notes on tower fire.

GROUP 7, 2:30–3 P.M. Tower Personnel

Comments on the fire–fighting equipment used in the fire a few days ago. They include:

1. The water hoses in the area of the fire were inadequate. They should be two-inch lines.
2. The extinguishers were available, but a lot of things were stored tightly around some of them; there was difficulty in getting them freed.
3. A better source of water is needed in the area where the fire occurred. Is such a better source also needed on the fourth and fifth floors? They think the answer would be yes.
4. The fire was detected between 12 noon and 12:30 P.M. But it was almost impossible to get an outside telephone line: "Someone was using our phones." Also, some men had to knock down a gate to get out of the tower area. They were unable to get out through the shed.
5. Should there be a hand alarm system covering the plant premises?
6. The water line behind the dryers hasn't been checked for months. It should be checked regularly.
7. A wall should be put up to block off the conveyor from the dryers. The wall would be a safety measure. It could be a simple partition.

Wednesday

"Did the change in the suction system on your router have any effect on the dust situation at the machine?" Byrne asked.

"I don't know," Mike Tortorello, mill operator, said. "It seems as if it did. It's a lot easier to stay at the job—you don't have to go away coughing and choking every few minutes. Anyway, they *tried.*"

Worker's comments revealed another phenomenon: Some distortion was built in. Many workers and some foremen were talking different languages. Prisoners of the plant's history of strife, they still held to false shibboleths affecting behavior.

Wednesday

"Look at this," Byrne said. "Here's a worker in Extrusion who says the foremen are all over him all the time—the foremen have too much authority. . .there are too many of them. . .you can't work for three of them at once—this is his pitch. And a foreman in the same department says no one backs him up, no one gives him any real authority, only responsibility. He's suggesting that we put some instructions into the policy manual on how foremen get gold-bricks to do a day's work."

"Are there other things like that?" Gallery asked. "Are there any concepts or attitudes that may actually be holding us up?"

"There are a number of them. I think you could actually attack this problem, but in face-to-face meetings. This is too sensitive to be done in writing."

"Can you give me a list? That's one of the things I want to go into in my state-of-the-plant talks."

So began Gallery's frontal attack on concept barriers, blocks, filters, frozen attitudes.

Monday

"Fellow employees," Gallery began, "we have a problem here. I want to ask your help in solving it. Together, I believe we *can* solve it. The problem isn't so much one of physical difficulties at the workplace. Not any longer. We're working at that kind of problem. We've done a lot already. The problem now is one of attitude. I'd like to ask each of you to consider some of the attitudes—the slogans and twisted concepts—that are hurting us. This goes for some of us in management—foremen and others—as well as for some hourly employees."

Gallery turned up the blank top sheet of a flip chart. On the undersheet were listed a number of items in large letters:

Poor Management Attitudes, Methods	*Poor Worker Attitudes, Methods*
Combat psychology	Let George do it
Pushing, not leading	It costs the company, not me
It's not in my bailiwick	Tendency to overreact
"I'll tell you what you need to know—and no more"	Take a chance on quality
Take a chance on quality	Show me money, then I'll do better
Failure to inform in advance	Management has too many *rights*, no *duties*

That first Fab group listened to Gallery carefully. He went from his initial problem analysis through a complete rundown of how the plant was doing financially and operationally: better, but not yet satisfactory. He called for new thinking. When he finished, his audience clapped. "We should have had something like this long ago," one worker told him later.

Gallery went through the plant, area by area, department by department, giving his basic talk. The task took four weeks.

Two months later, in April, Fabricating shipped over $1.5 million in goods, more than ever before in its 50-year history. Other departments showed substantial, if less spectacular, improvement.

THE HOUSE THAT GEORGE BUILT

Gallery had blown air through the entire organization. He had opened windows of communication. He had spoken frankly of problems. His program did not end there, but caught on and moved faster. Foremen and department managers began to find ingenious ways to meet motivational needs.

Tuesday

The five extrusion setup men sit uneasily in Al Moroney's glassed-in office. They don't know why they've been called in; Moroney hasn't had time to tell them. But now Al walks into the office smiling and sets them at ease with a few words.

"I don't know whether you guys heard," he says, "but we're considering a new type of extruder. From what we've heard, it's a real beaut. But we want to check that out. I've gotten top management's OK to send one foreman and one setup man down to the manufacturer's plant to look this thing over and report back to me. The question is, who? You're all about equally qualified."

Suddenly the men are talking, making suggestions.

Responsibility, recognition, achievement, growth are in the air: behind them cooperative planning, problem solving, involvement, free flow of information—all the pillars on which genuine, committed participation is built.

So Gallery saw it and so he kept working at it. He made arrangements for foremen to take training, on a voluntary basis, in human relations and communications. The program was announced in a memo that quoted an authority in the management field: "Every manager realizes that communications makes an organization run. But not every manager realizes that *how* he communicates determines *how well* the organization runs."*

Other efforts followed steadily: A picnic in August helped close the 20-year-old social gap between management and workers; a communications policy (Exhibit 1-7) went into the Foreman's Policy Manual; volunteer workers and foremen manned a plant booth, side by side, at a local "quality" fair.

Merv Hargit resigned a month after the picnic, taking early retirement. His tone, his words had never changed; he sounded more and more like a voice from a long-closed grave.

Tuesday

"This is great, Merv," Gallery said. Grievances down by half in eight months."

"They're just waiting in the weeds to sandbag us."

Friday

"We're going to add some very gentle guidance on our philosophy of discipline to the policy manual, Merv," Gallery said.

"No one'll read it—no one."

Gallery, in his office with Byrne, sketched new plans. You had to keep moving. A changed approach required continuous

---

*Ralph W. Crosby, *Person-to-Person Management* (Philadelphia and New York: Chilton Books, Publishers, 1966), p. 16.

1-7. Communications policy, Foreman's Policy Manual.

I. Our desire is to encourage good, effective communication. This means the timely interchange of facts, ideas, and opinions that help inform, achieve understanding, and create attitudes that lead to best results on the job.

II. If communication in our plant is to be effective, we believe all personnel should participate. Supervisors in particular are to be included in the internal communications fabric. The reason is that supervisors are generally seen as key links in the communications chain as in operational areas.

III. Our aims in furthering good communication may be itemized as follows:

A. To have all personnel understand, appreciate, and accept the need for good communication.

B. To help all personnel feel the satisfaction that comes from (a) having a common purpose and (b) being a part of a joint effort.

C. To encourage a communications-conscious attitude, with each individual asking, "Who else should know about this? And what is the best way of getting it to him?"

D. To keep every employee informed, to the greatest degree possible, on all company matters that directly or indirectly affect him.

E. To make certain that all personnel understand, as thoroughly as possible, the purposes, objectives, policies, rules, plans, and programs of the plant and company.

F. To insure that all personnel understand the why as well as the how of their jobs.

G. To enable all employees to understand and recognize their opportunities and responsibilities for pulling together.

H To make it possible for the plant and company to stand high in the estimation of its own employees, the public, and the community.

1-7 (Cont.)

I. To insure that communication, as such, is two-way and that all questions or suggestions are given full consideration.

J. To have lines of communication that are as short and direct as possible.

---

movement, unending elaboration. A new policy had to be followed by action that made it real. Workers in an entire plant could, as at Hawthorne on a more limited scale, be made aware of a new climate; they could be given a sense of management concern that would encourage greater effort. In this one plant at least, years of conflict had not obliterated the basic drive of the workforce to work well and to take pride in good work.

Listening had produced a Hawthorne effect.

2

The Foreman:
Where the Buck Stops

JIM! WHERE THE HELL are those castings for the Marchant job? Don't you know they wanted them day before yesterday?"

Joe Anderson, plant manager of The Barr Iron Works, was starting to walk through the castings department when he heard that roar. He decided it wasn't a good time to talk to Jim Caldwell as he'd intended, so he retreated; but he heard the beginning of Jim's apology to George Husted, area foreman. "Sorry, George. I've been leaning on these guys till they're about to fall over."

Anderson didn't hear the rest.

Anderson had been responsible for making Jim foreman of the castings department. For years the division had promoted skilled workmen to foremen's jobs as the incumbents retired. Sometimes it worked out and sometimes it didn't. Too often the company had lost the production of one of its best workmen only to gain a foreman who created as many problems as he solved.

Jim Caldwell belonged to a new breed. He hadn't come up the hard way; he had taken his basic training in college. Then after a year and a half as an assistant foreman, learning the ropes and doing the paperwork for one of the older men, he had been put in charge.

The promotion had been Anderson's idea. He had laid his own prestige on the line to sell it to his crusty boss, Edwin Meyer, works manager and the parent RJB Corporation's top banana on these premises. But there had been endless trouble in the castings department ever since. It wasn't curing itself with time, as Anderson had thought it might. In fact, it seemed to be getting worse. Even so, Anderson wasn't ready to give up just yet. He still thought Caldwell had potential, so late that same afternoon Anderson asked him to come in.

"Jim, sit down. It's time we went into a huddle on some problems." He could see Jim stiffen a little at the mention of the word "problems." He went on talking to ease the tension so Jim would talk.

A LITANY OF PROBLEMS

"We all have problems, Jim. I'm supposed to be a problem solver. So are you. That's what management is all about. If there weren't any problems, the company wouldn't need us. Now I think you've been in charge of the castings department long enough to know that the company needs all your brains and all your training to help solve some of our problems.

"But it needs more than that. No problem of this company is yours alone or mine alone. If any of us falls on his face, it's everybody's hard luck. Anyway, you've had a little time to get the feel of being foreman of the castings department, and I wish you'd give me your thoughts on what the specific problems are. Maybe we can help each other get on top of them."

Jim wasn't entirely relaxed, but he gave it a try.

"Problems?" he grunted. "I've got nothing but problems. I seem to be right in the middle. If the men in the department aren't blasting me because I'm younger than they are and am supposed to know more, I'm taking the heat from some other department. The work isn't flowing to them the way they want it, or another department is holding me up so I can't deliver when I'm supposed to. It's one thing after another. If we're delivering on time, Accounting comes in with a beef about the cost of overtime."

Anderson gave him a commiserating grin. "Sounds like all the bucks stop at your desk. It didn't sound that way in those lecture courses in business administration, did it?" He waited a minute for an answer, but Jim only said no.

Anderson took the ball again. "Well, we're in this together. Let's see if we can take these problems one at a time. They're interrelated, of course. All our problems start with people. But let's tackle the first one: The men in the department resent you because you're younger and are supposed to know more. Can you give me an example?"

"I've got nothing but examples. I could spend the day telling you. Well, take Andy Baker. It all seems to start with him."

"Andy? That surprises me. He's always been a first-class workman, and company-minded, too. I wouldn't think you'd have much trouble with Andy. What's the problem?"

"He *is* a first-class workman. Best in the plant. In fact, all the men go to him with their production problems instead of coming to me. Sure he knows his job. But all the men think he should have been made foreman, and so does he. How do you fight city hall?"

"Can you get him on your side? Can you ask him what gives?"

"*Ask* him?" Jim swallowed. "I just can't see that, with all the men waiting to join in whatever response he chooses to make, whether he laughs or clams up or spits in my eye. He might even put on a nancy walk and voice and pretend he was mimicking me: 'Andy, dear, please show me how to hemstitch this hanky.' Right there I'd lose the ball game. They'd all be laughing behind their hands."

Anderson had a momentary impulse to make a speech. A management man, he felt like saying, has to be big enough to get on top of that sort of thing. But he resisted the urge to preach. Jim was young yet, and if Anderson hoped to make the most of him, he'd have to let the fledgling manager grow at his own pace, with whatever guidance an older hand could offer.

"Sounds like you need a referee," Anderson said, smiling, "and I guess I'm it. After all, it was my idea to bring in college-trained foremen. But it was an experiment, of course. It still is. Actually, Andy Baker is as much a guinea pig as you are. We wanted to see how the men would react to a college man. Maybe I should have done a better job of preparing the men for the new deal in foremen. Do you suppose I could break down this wall for you by talking to Andy?"

Jim shrugged. "I don't know. You're probably a better miracle worker than I am."

"Well, if you think you can ask him to come in without making him madder than he already is, I'll give it a try." Anderson rose and stretched out his hand. "Take it easy, Jim," he said. "Rome wasn't built in a day, and neither was this company."

"OK," Jim said.

"Do me two favors. First, get a copy of a book you've probably read already and check a chart in it. Make a copy of the chart and carry it around with you. The book is by Uris and Shapin—*Working with People**—and the chart suggests ways to overcome personality resistance, which is just what you're encountering."

*Auren Uris and Betty Shapin, *Working with People* (New York: The Macmillan Company, 1953), pp. 112-113.

Anderson wrote down the name of the book and the description of the chart. (The chart is shown in Exhibit 2-1.) "That's favor No. 1," he said. "No. 2 may be a little harder. I want you to invent for me a way to prove to everyone in this plant that what you said earlier about Baker is true, that he's the best worker in the plant. Think you can do it?"

"I don't know—"

"Do you believe it?"

"I certainly do."

"Then you'll find a way. Can you send Baker in now?"

RESISTANCE ROCK

When Andy Baker set his mind, Joe Anderson knew, it clamped shut almost audibly. Baker could be resistance rock itself. Now it appeared he had set his mind: When he walked in, he was obviously on guard.

"Hi, Andy," the plant manager said. "Have a seat. It's been quite a while since we've had a chance to talk. How's it going?"

"OK, I guess."

Anderson realized that he wasn't going to melt this worker's reserve with the "How are you? I'm fine" routine. Baker was a pretty sharp observer, and would know he had been the subject of conversation between Anderson and Caldwell. Anderson decided to wade right in.

"I need your advice, Andy," he began. "You've been with this company a long time and know a lot of its problems as well as I do—some of them better. I know your brains aren't all in your hands. You've got eyes and ears, too, and you know we're having problems in the castings department. I'd like your slant on them. What gives?"

"Why don't you ask Caldwell?" Andy retorted.

"I did." Anderson laughed. "I want it from you."

2-1. How to overcome personality resistance.

	ORDERS	UNJUSTIFIED COMPLAINTS	PRAISE	CORRECTION	CHANGE
Stubborn	Use requests most of the time—"Would you please take this to the store room?"—but don't hesitate to show authority if he balks—"Down to the store room with this, Joe. Do it first, and if you like, we'll discuss it later."	Don't try to make him admit he's wrong. Sell him your decision on the basis of fairness to all. "To give you what you want would be unfair to the others, Joe. And you know I run this department on an impartial basis."	Praise any signs of cooperation. It's an effort on his part to change his mental attitude. "The boys appreciate your pitching in. And so do I. Nice work."	He'll never admit he did wrong. Concentrate on showing him the right way and how to do it. Discuss faults as problems for him to lick. "You've got perseverance, Joe. You can win out if you make up your mind to it."	He won't accept change easily. Point up advantages. Sell him with facts keyed to his viewpoints. "This is close to what you were telling me a few days ago, Joe. Let's see whether you were wrong or right."
Slow	Give him time to digest an order before you expect it carried out. Talk slowly. Pause between points. Ask him to repeat.	He mulls over gripes a long time, they're apt to be important to him. Show him you think them important, need time to consider.	Always praise when he steps up his normal speed. It's a big effort for him, he's really trying. Praise seriously, make it an important matter.	Make it straight from the shoulder but friendly. Don't ruffle him by a rapid-fire approach. And give him time to re-adjust himself.	Sell him on a change first and as far in advance as possible. Make your explanations complete, leave nothing to his imagination.
Sensitive	Phrase as suggestions as much as possible: "I think that's about finished now. Don't you agree?"	He's apt to blow them up. Reassure him as to your continued friendliness. "Glad you talked it over with me now. Makes my job easier when you come to me like that."	Give praise often. He responds very well to it. More than any other type, he flourishes in an atmosphere of approval.	He'll be impressed by slight criticism, depressed by too much. Stress ability to improve—"With your ability I know you can do better. Suppose you take a bit more time to check."	Give him individual reassurance. He's apt to be worried by change. "This is to help speed things up for accounting." Emphasize the reasons for change.

2-1 (Cont.)

Timid	Spell out what you want done clearly. He won't ask questions, so get him to repeat to make sure he understands—"Would you run through that for me so I can see if I've remembered everything?"	He won't come up to you with complaints. In any extreme cases, it's up to you to anticipate. Question him directly or ask leading questions that create the opportunity for him to unload.	Praise him for using initiative, overcoming difficulties himself. It's tough for him—"I like the way you handled that rush order. No one could have done it better."	When possible, play down seriousness of fault. "This isn't terribly important, but I know you'll want to take care of it." Lard heavily with praise—"You're doing such a swell job it will be easy for you to tighten up on this small matter." Reassure as to continued good feeling after any criticism.	Bolster his security by showing how little change affects him. "This is just a minor shift in our way of doing things." Stress reasons larger than his own sphere — "We figure we can process orders faster, which gives the firm an edge over its competitors."
Bold	Phrase as requests. Stress reliance on his responsibility—"I know I can count on you to get this done." But check for rashness, lack of thinking through.	He's apt to complain just to assert himself. He can be kidded out of it, in man-to-man fashion. "Sure, Bill, all the out-of-date equipment is specially marked to be given to you. But I notice you're doing a pretty good job with the antiquated stuff."	He's apt to take praise as his due. Praise only for something outstanding. Be brief. "Nice work Bill." He'll resent anything he thinks is soft soap. But make it quite clear that you're impressed by his accomplishment.	It's hard for him to believe he can do wrong. Be matter-of-fact. Speak quietly, don't let him argue.	He's a good one to lead off a change. "Bill, you like variety. Suppose you start this off and let's see how it goes."

Source: Auren Uris and Betty Shapin, *Working with People* (New York: The Macmillan Compnay, 1953), pp. 112-113.

That broke the tension. Baker grinned, too. "I don't know what you expect," he said, "bringing in these punks who think they know about castings because they went to college. Passing over men who have worked their tails off for you when a foreman's job opens up. You say I've got brains. Why the hell didn't you give me a chance to prove it?"

This was it, Anderson realized. Gloves off. He'd better play it slow and easy.

"To tell the truth," he said, "I didn't think you'd want it. You've put in a lot of time for us, lots of it overtime at time and a half or double time. And you've given value for every nickel of it. Don't think for a minute I don't know it. But a foreman doesn't get paid for overtime. . . ."

"I don't give a damn about the overtime," Andy cut in. "My kids are grown up. I've put them all through college, and I'd just as soon let the other guys have some of the overtime from now on. Maybe I could do with a little fishing."

"I like to fish, too," Anderson said, "but I don't get much time for it. The hell of it is, Andy, that when a man takes on a management job he still puts in the overtime—some of it lying awake nights worrying. He just doesn't get paid time and a half for it. Quite often Caldwell's paychecks aren't as big as yours. . . ." Anderson paused, letting that sink in. "So your kids are all through college, are they? Would you say they're 'punks' as you put it a minute ago, or did they learn something that was worth your hard-earned dough?"

"I don't know what they learned," Baker said mirthlessly. "Sometimes I think they'd have learned more if they got it the way I got it. But at least when the titles are passed around, they'll be at the head of the line like Caldwell, and their kids will be able to give back a big answer when someone asks them what their dad does, even if their dads' jobs don't take half the brains mine does."

So it was the title Andy wanted. His kids were involved.

Maybe his kids *were* punks, and had let their dad know a two-penny front-office title sounded better to them than skilled machinist. Maybe Andy had heard one of them hesitate or mumble when a friend asked, "What does your dad do?" This would take some thinking to solve, Anderson realized. But he could make a start, perhaps.

"Hell, Andy," he began, "I could give you a title. But why should I try to kid you with a title that didn't mean anything. I don't think I could. Besides, you're a damned valuable man. We need you right where you are."

"So I'm too valuable to promote? Maybe a guy shouldn't do his damnedest, should be satisfied if his work just gets by."

"You know better than that."

"I thought I did, but—well, it doesn't matter."

"It matters like hell. If the people who are satisfied just to get by ever outnumber those who do their damnedest, this company is in deep trouble."

TALK THERAPY

Suddenly Baker was talking, getting off his chest things that apparently had been bothering him for months, even years. As he talked, Anderson noticed, his mood settled. He became different. The monologue he was delivering was working some mysterious therapy inside him.

When they had finished, Baker shook Anderson's hand. "Great to talk to you, Joe," Baker said. "Why don't you get out on the floor more often? The guys all say they like it—you know, they want to feel management's interested."

"Will do."

With Baker gone, Anderson sat back. He had absorbed some information that would be of value to Caldwell. That business about putting two kids through college, and then finding that these kids think they're too hoity-toity for you.

There's a key to every man's inner heart, Anderson thought. The rest of that day he was lost in job details, but the next morning he got a call from Caldwell. During the night the foreman had worked out a plan to prove that Baker was the top worker in the plant, and he wanted to go over it with Anderson (see Exhibit 2-2).

This was crucial. Anderson decided to set aside the report he was working on; he could skip lunch and have it done on time anyway. "Come on up," he told Caldwell.

The foreman was nervous as he presented his plan. He pulled a wadded-up sheet of paper from his pocket and unfolded it. Anderson took it.

"Take a chair, Jim." He read the notes, set them on the desk.

"This is terrific," Anderson said. "This is the kind of thing we're looking for. Do you mind if I probe your thinking a little more?"

Caldwell was relaxed, pleased. "That's what I'm here for."

"How do you know, first of all, that Baker would be the choice if we launched this plan?"

"He'd win it hands down."

"We couldn't have a fix."

"I know. That would kill the whole scheme. It's got to be done straight. I'd be willing to put money on Baker."

"I'm going to go over this idea with Ed. I may also get some of the other foremen in on it. I may even let them think it was their idea. Would you mind that, Jim?"

"Not at all. I have no special pride of authorship."

"Great. Let's take a few more minutes to talk about Baker." Anderson went over what he had heard the preceding day, not betraying a confidence but trying to put Baker's personal situation into perspective. Caldwell didn't miss a single word.

2-2. Caldwell's plan.

1. Since we're coming up to the end of the year, announce a Worker of the Year contest. Everyone in the plant would vote, by department, for the man he considered to be the best worker.

2. With seven men selected as above, one for each of the seven departments, to take part in the finals of the Worker of the Year competition, a committee would have a week to make a single, final selection. The committee would be composed of a line management representative (if possible Mr. Anderson), a man from Personnel, and three workers to be selected at random.

3. The committee would make the final selection on the basis of the man's work record, attendance record, production achievements if such could be reduced to figures, commendations issued before the date the competition was announced, seniority, and so on.

4. With a single man chosen as the Worker of the Year, the broadest possible publicity would be given to the individual. He would be taken to lunch by Mr. Meyer. He would represent the plant the following spring at the areawide Quality Show. Most important of all, he would be honored at the plant Christmas party.

5. A similar competition would be run the following year, with the first man so honored serving as outgoing Man of the Year and receiving some new honors.

THE PSYCHEDELIC CONTEST

If psychedelic meant mind-opening, or mind-bending, this competition was going to be it, Anderson decided. He began to prepare the groundwork for it, with Ed Meyer, works manager, and the entire foreman group. He wanted maximum benefit from it.

Things simmered down a little in the castings department. Once or twice when he walked through, Anderson even saw Caldwell and Baker talking over the work together, if not amiably at least with what appeared to be mutual respect. And the work was going better, unquestionably.   But Anderson was still mulling over the central problem: how to make a good worker feel important and at the same time make others want to do the kind of job that would make them feel important too. There had to be some other way to do it besides the prospect of becoming foremen. There weren't enough foremen's jobs, and never would be, for all the men.   And of course, Anderson wanted to make good workmen out of all of them.

Besides, being a foreman took a different set of skills. Some good workmen had them. Some could develop them. But a lot of precious skill went to waste when some of them traded the workbench for a desk and a file cabinet. Not always, of course. Some of them went right on being good workmen instead of giving their attention to planning the work and getting other men to carry out the plans. Mort Higgins was one of them. A fine workman who loved his tools, he'd had a devil of a time trying to lay them down, and he'd never become more than a mediocre foreman. What a waste. And there was no way to reclaim the good workman they'd lost. A demotion would have killed the guy, and it wouldn't have been fair to make him pay with his pride for someone else's mistake. So they'd worked around him, giving him what help they could.

Pride. Dammit, a good workman had a right to it. And no college-trained punk had any call to look down his nose at a Mort Higgins or an Andy Baker. Wait till these kids of Baker's could do *any* kind of job as well as those men did the jobs they'd spent their lives doing. Then let them strut, if they ever made it.

Each foreman had his own style, had to have it. Bill Parsons had been one of the best-liked men in the maintenance department, and one the others genuinely respected. When he took the foreman's job, he tried so hard to please everybody that he wound up unable to please anybody—until an exchange of views at a foreman's meeting made him realize that the men in his department didn't really want to be babied or bullied. Matt Taylor was the kind who tried so hard to be the boss that he was overassertive with the men who had been his pals. Anderson remembered what Matt had said at one meeting: "What's the problem? Either they shape up or they don't. You just tell 'em and don't take any back talk."

One of Taylor's men had argued that what Taylor called "back talk" sometimes might yield a good idea if a foreman listened. Furthermore, the man said, the foreman wasn't the only one with brains in the department. Taylor was learning that slowly, but he still acted pretty much like a top sergeant.

THE MEETING

Anderson called a foreman's meeting to tell them about the contest. He wanted to hear those men discuss ways to help employees develop pride in their work.

It was quite a session. The men started out with questions. "Who are we trying to kid? All those guys want is a paycheck." Another argued that the jobs in his department were dull and that there was no way to make them seem important. But when a top man like Jack Hanischer said, "Oh, I don't know," to one such comment and then told of a case or two in which even a dull job done right had proved to be very important indeed, the other foremen began to think of experiences of their own.

One concrete idea came out of it, though it had been in Anderson's mind when the meeting started. He had waited, serving as moderator and not talking much, while the men exchanged experiences and learned from each other, till the skeptical ones were ready to say, at least, "Well, maybe."

"I was thinking about some kind of awards program," Anderson said then. A contest choosing the most valuable man of the month or the year—something like that. Giving substantial prizes, getting some publicity in the town paper and on TV, making the men feel that it's an honor to be a good worker and that we know they're there. What do you think?"

"Who would choose them?" Mike Thompson asked.

"I've been thinking that over. If the men were to choose, we'd have a good opportunity to open some minds as to what makes a worker valuable to a company. It might make them think a little more about the value of their own contribution and how to make it a good one. That's a good word to get thinking about, by the way—*contribution*. They all make a contribution. It won't hurt to let them know it."

"Sweep the floor pretty, Jo-Jo," Tom Ross, who considered himself the company wit, put in. "It's a valuable contribution."

"You're damn right it is," Bill Parsons asserted. "I got my heel caught once in a hunk of old chewing gum and took a header down a flight of stairs."

Anderson cut in, shutting off the obvious wisecracks about Bill's fall on his head. "I don't think any of us can belittle the value of good housekeeping," he said. "The whole point is that we must not—repeat, must not—belittle anyone's work.

If the company didn't need the work of every man on the payroll—and need it done well—some men wouldn't be on the payroll. Even the dullest job is an important job. It's important that it be done right. We've got to stop belittling and start building. We want our men saying and thinking, 'I take care of the floors so no one will fall,' not that they're 'just' janitors or 'just' anything else."

SELF-ESTEEM: THE TARGET FOR TODAY

Anderson took out a sheet of paper covered with notes (see Exhibit 2-3). "I consider this so important that I'm going to give you guys a list of suggestions on building a worker's self-esteem. This is from a book—I didn't invent it. I think it bears directly on what we're talking about. I'll get a copy to each of you. In the meantime, think about a competition that will do the same thing in a dramatic way that you're trying to do every minute you spend on the floors."

POPULAR CHOICE

Things turned out just as Caldwell had predicted. The competition was held, the men voted, the committee selected the winner—and Baker won in a walk.

The Christmas party traditionally was managed buffet-style. Some men brought their wives and kids. Because Barr Iron Works was the town's largest employer, both the local newspaper and the TV station were interested when Anderson told them what was planned.

Andy Baker's wife came, as she always did, but his boys thought they were too big for it. They were surprised when they caught their dad on TV and heard the speeches Anderson and Caldwell made about him: "Most valuable," "Real contribution," "Passing on to the younger men not only his

2-3. Do's and don'ts in building employee self-esteem.

TREAT AN EMPLOYEE AS AN INDIVIDUAL

Don't	*Do*
Ignore employee	Notice employee
• Ignore suggestions	• Encourage suggestions
• Keep employee waiting	• Keep appointments promptly
Treat impersonally	Call employee by name
Show no interest	Draw out in conversation
Break promises	Keep all promises

GIVE DESERVED RECOGNITION

Don't	*Do*
Fail to give credit when due	Be prompt in giving credit
Praise results only	Recognize effort as well as achievement
Blame unfairly	Be cautious in placing blame
Fail to see potentialities	Encourage initiative and talent
Fail to let employee know progress	Let employee know how he is doing

AVOID BELITTLING

Don't	*Do*
	Treat employee as co-worker, not inferior
Assume the "boss" attitude	
• Boast of one's position	• Allow employee to express opinions
• Assume superior attitude	• Talk *with*, not *at*, employee
• Dictate	• Suggest
• Speak in a loud voice	• Speak in moderate tones
• Use fear as a weapon	• Avoid use of threats
Appear too busy to listen	Take time to listen attentively
Criticize thoughtlessly	Criticize tactfully
• Criticize in public	• Criticize in private
• Criticize personally	• Be objective and impersonal
• Criticize only negatively	• Criticize constructively
• Nag	• Allow employee to correct own mistakes
• Withhold criticism when needed	• Give criticism when needed
Anticipate failure	Make employee feel he will succeed
Use sarcasm or ridicule	Avoid playing up oneself at employee's expense

sharply honed skills but the integrity that wouldn't let him do less than his best when others might be satisfied just to get by."

The boys listened to the phrases. "God, sounds like a funeral oration," the older one said, but he was impressed in spite of himself. "Think anyone ever will say anything like that about you?" he asked his brother.

THE SENSE OF PROGRESS

Anderson heard about that later. He was busy awarding the prize: a week's fishing trip off the coast of Florida with all expenses paid for Mr. and Mrs. Baker. Andy came back with a tan, and Caldwell was the first to greet him.

Now Joe Anderson got the feeling that the same thing was happening in all the departments, but mostly in castings. He would have to find ways to keep it going. That was the thing. This couldn't be a one-shot deal. Now that a few minds had been opened a little, he had to keep them open. And that included both the foremen and the men they supervised.

Would a suggestion box program be a good followup, he wondered, or would it be better just to invite suggestions informally, as they always had—*or had they?*

That would be a good topic for another foreman's meeting. It would start them talking and thinking. The thinking was the main thing, of course. If the men kept their eyes, ears, and minds open and realized that the company needed from them not only their production but their ideas as well, their respect for themselves and their jobs would increase, and benefits to the company would have to follow.

How that would pay off on the balance sheet, only

Accounting could tell him, and it would take a while to see improvement in those terms. And of course there were always other factors involved, which made it impossible to measure the effect of a program like this.

But there already had been some effect. Castings, for example, hadn't shipped late in six weeks.

3

The Self-Imposed Production Limitation

WALK ALONG BOLTON STREET, which hangs halfway up the hill rising steeply from the Mississippi River. Cross Fenton and continue on. Beyond Rosie's Grill is a paint factory that blocks the view of the RJB Corporation's Fabricating Division plant.

Pass both the grill and the ancient, decrepit paint factory and enter the RJB plant by the side door used by employees. On the left of the door as you enter stands a bank of vending machines containing soda, hot coffee, candy and gum, and other staples of vending operations. Walk down the wide aisle leading straight away from the door: Thirty yards along here you pass through a fire door, entering an extension of the building. Machines set in a double line are making a variety of wheezing, humming, and thumping sounds. The machines throw off gray smoke that rises rapidly, and although the ceiling is high, the air seems perpetually clouded.

Leading off to the right is another, narrower aisle. Walk down it. A wooden storage bin stands on the right, full of assorted junk. Beyond the bin is the wall of a "white room" enclosed by glass windows. Twenty feet farther down the aisle rises a brick wall. You are in a dead end.

The words "Rip out the Berlin Wall!" have been scrawled in huge letters on the whitewashed surface. Below that message, in smaller letters, you read: "Or tube production goes down to 800 a day."

MANAGEMENT BY EXCEPTION

The word went around quickly. An hour after the paint had been splashed on the wall, Gene O'Dell, department manager in the tube department, stood in front of the dead end with his second-shift foreman, Mike Malvern. O'Dell looked grim; Malvern was plain mad.

"Why don't we just paint over it?" Malvern asked.

"Too late. The honcho's on the way down. He wants to see it."

"Why? This ain't nothin'. These guys are always pullin' somethin' like this."

"You know that and I know it," O'Dell said, "but Roney wants to see it."

"At five-thirty in the afternoon?"

"At five-thirty in the afternoon. Roney never goes home, you know that."

They were still talking when Roney, the plant manager, appeared. He noted the message, spoke briefly with O'Dell, a tall, rangy man, and Malvern, shorter and stockier. Roney, sandy-haired and with blazing eyes, about two inches taller than Malvern, asked the inevitable question: "Who did it?"

Malvern answered. "Probably Gallarneau. He's been makin' a lot of trouble lately."

"It's two different handwritings if you ask me," said Roney. "Also, Gallarneau's a steward. Would you suggest that a steward would do this?"

"Sure would," Malvern said.

Roney was curt. "Let's go to the office."

The three men walked through the department. The men working at the dozen or so tube-making machines looked up as they passed, then bent quickly to their work again. In a couple of instances pairs of them at parallel machines glanced over at each other.

Inside the office, with the glass door closed, Roney asked some pointed questions. He knew what the department's record was: Tube production had been going down, or at best standing at a level, for at least two years. He himself had appointed O'Dell to the job of department manager to "clean up down there" and no improvement had been forthcoming. The department manager always had an excuse, and now Jesse Roney heard it all again:

□ Sure, tube production was going down despite some mechanical innovations that should have doubled it; but the men were fighting the company down here. They always had, always would.

□ Strenuous efforts had been exerted to get the men on the ball, to no avail. A week ago, O'Dell had talked to all three shifts, really laying it on the line. No change.

□ The foremen were doing a good job, Malvern and Piatek, the day foreman, in particular. Kennelley, third-shift foreman, was showing up as too soft on his people. Yes, his shift turned out 1,100 tubes and more, per man per shift, but that was the night shift—it wasn't as pro-union as the other two shifts.

□ All three foremen had been told to hound the machine operators and others, to put an end to goldbricking, to get production up come what might.

□ When a man screwed up, he really got a chewing.

To Roney, it sounded like management by exception and he said so: "That's when you only communicate with your people if something goes wrong."

A WALL AS COMMUNICATION

Roney wouldn't let it drop. He appeared without warning in the department during any of the three shifts. He talked to some of the men. He talked to all three foremen, individually, collectively, in pairs at shift changes. He was told, very early, that the wall had been erected by agreement between O'Dell and the department manager in the oven area, the adjoining department.

"We had to do something about that corridor," O'Dell said. "The men were going through it to the vending machines in the oven area—they're closer than the ones by the side entrance. Also, you can get to them fast, and get away fast. But the aisle down there was always cluttered with garbage. Cigarettes, paper cups, pieces of sandwiches—God, we must really have rats. A building this old. Joe and I decided that we had to cut it off. Joe was really mad about the mess our guys were leaving in his department."

Roney didn't care about how mad Joe was. "Haven't you just compounded the department's problems?" he said. "Look, you're down here in the rectum of creation, with smoke in the air, grime on the walls, noise, tubes on the floor that people could trip on, a union group—all oldtimers—that's at war with management. Your men are combined against you. Doesn't that indicate you need some creative solutions?"

"These guys won't stand creativity."

"You're not asking them to stand it. You're going to give it to them."

KNOW THY PEOPLE

This time Roney showed up with a piece of paper. "I've got a checklist here," he said. "It comes from a book. I wonder if we could use it to characterize the people in the department, and work from there."

"Jesse, I know these people—" O'Dell was nettled, and trying not to show it. "OK, let's look at it."

Roney tossed the sheet on the desk. It bore the title "Characteristics of hygiene-oriented and work-oriented personnel." It showed various items listed in double columns (see Exhibit 3-1).

O'Dell began to read. Comprehension spread over his face as his eyes moved down the page. "Where'd you get this, Jesse? This lefthand column describes our guys perfectly. They're all of these things—they show little interest in the quality of their work, they don't profit professionally from experience, they're. . .cynical."

"All of them, on all three shifts?"

O'Dell thought. "Maybe not on the third shift. Kennelley's got those guys buffaloed."

"They're motivation seekers? Not hygiene seekers? All of them? You know them, Gene. Are they?"

The challenge of the whole line of thought had become puzzling to O'Dell. He was torn between the urge to give the stock answer and the need to answer honestly in this new situation. "Well, they used to be just the same as the other men, but like I said, Kennelley's—"

"Nuts! Kennelley doesn't have them buffaloed," Roney shot back. "He's doing something right. I want you to find out what it is. Now, do you understand what that hygiene business is about?"

"Well—."

" 'Hygiene' refers to the working conditions. This whole idea of hygiene seekers and motivation seekers was worked out by a guy named Herzberg. It means some workers are more attuned to the working conditions than to the work itself. Where the conditions are bad, and stay bad over a long period of time, the people tend to get lost in their own problems. There are others who have done some thinking on this subject. They believe the company is responsible when this happens."

3-1. Characteristics of hygiene-oriented and work-oriented personnel.

HYGIENE SEEKER	MOTIVATION SEEKER
1. Motivated by nature of the environment.	1. Motivated by nature of the task.
2. Chronic and heightened dissatisfaction with various aspects of his job context, e.g., salary, supervision, working conditions, status, job security, company policy and administration, fellow employees.	2. Higher tolerance for poor hygiene factors.
3. Overreaction to improvement in hygiene factors.	3. Less reaction to improvement in hygiene factors.
4. Short duration of satisfaction when hygiene factors are improved.	4. Short duration of satisfaction when hygiene factors are improved.
5. Overreaction when hygiene factors are not improved.	5. Milder discontent when hygiene factors need improvement.
6. Realizes little satisfaction from accomplishments.	6. Realizes great satisfaction from accomplishments.
7. Shows little interest in the kind and quality of the work he does.	7. Has the capacity to enjoy the work he does.
8. Expresses cynicism regarding positive virtues of work and life in general.	8. Expresses positive feelings toward work and life in general.
9. Does not profit professionally from experience.	9. Profits professionally from experience.
10. Prone to cultural noises (a) Ultraliberal, ultraconservative. (b) Parrots management philosophy. (c) Acts more like top management than top management does.	10. Has the belief that management systems are sincere and considered.
11. May succeed on the job because of talent.	11. May be an overachiever.

Source: Frederick Herzberg, *Work and the Nature of Man* (Cleveland and New York: The World Publishing Co., 1971), p. 90.

"Are you suggesting that we've—"

"Yes. Now I want you to start talking to these guys. Really talking. Listening. Take a week. Then I want you to give me a list of the department's problems *as the men see them.* Got that?" O'Dell was nodding. Roney continued: "In the meantime, please have this notice typed up and posted. It's to tell the men I'm behind all this."

O'Dell watched Roney scribbling. Half an hour later O'Dell had posted the notice on the department bulletin board (see Exhibit 3-2).

THE BRAINWASHING

It was tough. Tougher than anything O'Dell had yet tackled. It violated his sense of propriety; his foremen, or two of them, said little, but reproach was written in their eyes, and O'Dell himself felt as if he were being brainwashed by his own subordinates.

The men did not hold back, nor did they butter their comments to make them palatable. But their mood remained one of inquiry, even if a strain of barely noticeable self-satisfaction ran beneath it.

O'Dell followed Roney's suggestions to the letter. He kept his mouth shut. When he saw Roney a week later, he had talked to men on all three shifts. He had boiled down the literally hundreds of comments he had received, coming out with a list of half a dozen items:

Maintenance

Housekeeping

Supervision

Communications, especially on
the department's status

The bonus system

Safety

3-2. Roney's memo to tube department personnel.

MEMORANDUM

TO ALL PERSONNEL, TUBE DEPARTMENT

We want to ask your help. We believe we need a brand-new look at the problems and challenges of the Tube Department. With your help and suggestions I think we can give the department a whole new lease on life.

Gene O'Dell will be talking to as many of you as possible over the next week or two. Please feel free to give Gene any ideas or comments on the department and its operations that you think will help us. Then Gene and I will go over all the ideas and get answers back to you.

We don't expect miracles. But we do promise to take action on your ideas wherever we can.

Jesse Roney
Plant Manager

"No mention of the Berlin Wall?" Roney asked as he ran his eye down the list.

"Plenty of them. I didn't know where to put those."

"Make them a separate category." Roney scribbled "Remove Berlin Wall" at the bottom of the list. "Now where do you go?" Roney asked.

O'Dell scratched his head. "I don't know. The way things have been going we don't have much of a budget for making improvements and changes."

"Would changes and improvements do any good?"

"I don't know. The men seem to be sincere enough."

"Then give me a requisition for a special allowance, listing the things you want to do with the dough. Put a paint job for the entire department near the top of your list. But don't expect miracles. I meant that when I wrote it in the bulletin board notice."

"What do you mean? We'd be going halfway to do what the men want."

"You'll still only be halfway. By fixing up the machines, you'll be killing an excuse for keeping production down. By fixing up the department, you'll be removing the source of a thousand other gripes. But there's a lot more to it than that."

Roney really began to talk. He had read the behavioral scientists and knew what he was talking about. He could break theory down into concrete applications. He also had a sense of proportion. "You're in a war here, you might as well recognize it," he said. "These men are deliberately keeping their production down, on the first and second shifts more than the third, but to some extent on the third as well. But this is a war you'll never win by frontal assault."

Victory would come only if O'Dell really got to understand his people, Roney said. O'Dell had taken the first step;

now a second had become necessary. Would O'Dell undertake it?

"Of course. Why not?"

"Because it's tougher than what you've done to date, and that's tough enough. I'm going to ask you to answer some questions about your people, either negatively or positively. Take another week. Research this carefully."

Roney dictated the questions from a notebook on his desk (see Exhibit 3-3). They were based, he said, on a series of assumptions that managements were *supposed* to be able to make regarding their employees in any situation.* Whether these assumptions could be made about this work group, Roney stressed, remained to be seen. He would not close his mind to the possibility that the situation might have deteriorated to the point where recovery might be impossible.

Once O'Dell had answered the questions, Roney indicated further, the next steps could be plotted. "Now what have I asked you to do?" he said.

O'Dell counted on his fingers. "Answer these questions. No. 1. Find out if the answers are more positive than negative. No. 2. Make recommendations to you for a special allowance to fix up the department."

"*If* the answers on the questions are favorable."

"Right. And No. 3. If we get the money, put the machines in shape and start working on the other things the men mentioned."

"Add a No. 4," Roney said. "Tell the men what you're doing as you go along. If you ask for money tell them you're asking me for money. If you start cleaning the place up, tell them you're starting to clean up."

*Douglas McGregor, *The Human Side of Enterprise* (New York: McGraw-Hill Book Co., 1960), pp. 47-48.

3.3 Roney's questions to O'Dell.

1. Are the men in Tube like others, or would they be under other circumstances, in the sense that they could or would expend physical and mental effort in work as naturally as in play?

2. Is it the case in Tube — keeping the third shift example in mind — that external or foreman control and the threat of punishment are the only means for bringing about effort toward organizational objectives — effort, for example, that would be exerted on an individual basis without regard to the production restriction?

3. Could the men in Tube be brought by some means as yet not found to commit themselves to company objectives, including higher productivity, through the introduction of rewards at some point? The rewards would be geared to produce job satisfaction and similar byproducts of constructive effort.

4. Is it possible that the men in Tube could learn in time not only to accept but to seek individual responsibility, including the responsibility for creativity, ingenuity, and similar characteristics, or are they far below average in these respects?

5. Are the capacities and innate talents of the men in Tube being only partially utilized?

THE MARKET SURVEY

Events and Roney's methods had begun to wrench O'Dell into new ways of thought. When he returned to report on the questions Roney had given him, he seemed more settled, less defensive. He had, clearly, done some hard thinking. Not the most intelligent of men, and generally somewhat visceral in his reactions, he had, this time, come to honest conclusions. All the questions could be answered positively, he said.

"You've thought this through?"

"Yes."

"You're telling me that these men can be rescued? That they're normal? That McGregor—the guy who devised those propositions I gave you—was right? You're telling me we should go on with this effort to turn the department around? That we should spend money where we're not making money? You understand this? You know, too, that we could close that department and be rid of a headache?"

"I know all that. I think we should try to save it. I think it can be made into a money-maker."

"Through the efforts of the men?"

"Exactly."

"Give me a program. Give me a specific amount that you'll need to get started. Let's go. Suddenly I'm excited."

O'Dell left. When he returned two days later, he had a request for special funds to accomplish a list of needed changes in the tube department. The priorities, he explained, had been worked out in consultation with the stewards and others in Tube, including the foremen.

"All three foremen?"

"Mostly Kennelley. Malvern and Piatek won't have much to do with all this."

Roney scanned the list of projects. Painting the department was there, high up, and so was complete maintenance overhaul of the tube-making machines, one machine at a time. A number of safety items were listed.

"All this will take some time even if we get a quick OK on the funds," O'Dell said. "Shouldn't we start on other things?"

"Like what?"

"We could tear out the Berlin Wall. I could talk the ovens people into it."

"No. Let's hold that as a kicker. It was a management action, one that we should assume was taken after serious thought, not whimsically. Let's not blow it off after a couple of weeks. When anyone asks you about it, say it's under discussion at a high level. It is. There's something else you could do, though."

"What's that?"

"Get your foremen on the first and second shifts to line up with what you're doing. They can wreck whatever you're trying to do."

O'Dell and Roney were thinking along parallel lines. They established an informal timetable for action in the tube department, seeking both removal or neutralization of demotivators and establishment of a positive climate in which job satisfaction would be a natural evolution.

O'Dell took the initiative in the department. He held the first of a series of monthly meetings to brief department employees on the business situation, the progress of efforts to obtain special maintenance and housekeeping funds, and other subjects. He used the bulletin board more often. Coming early and staying late, he worked with all three foremen, but with Piatek and Malvern more than Kennelley. The latter seemed to need no coaching or coaxing; he had a natural feel for human relations, and O'Dell began to watch him, actually to learn from him.

Roney came down into the department on a Tuesday. "Let's go through the department," he said to O'Dell.

As they walked, Roney got a progress report and delivered a few comments of his own. They nodded to the men as they went along; this was part of Roney's style. "Don't take too mechanistic a view of this process," he said. "Improving working conditions and communications—doing all the other things you're attempting—won't give you any guarantee of good results. Putting a machine into good running condition won't automatically guarantee you higher production. That remains a function of the worker's attitude in this kind of situation.

"There's another thing. Even with change and improvement, a better attitude won't develop along a straight, consistent line. It will more likely proceed in fits and starts."

"You're telling me we're dealing with people, not machines."

"Exactly." They had come back to the office. "Now for the news," Roney said as he sat down at O'Dell's desk. "We got half of what we asked for, so you can start on your extra maintenance and housekeeping work. Also, Tony, from Fabricating, is being assigned down here to do the special maintenance. He's going to be here on a temporary basis, but it may be fairly long term."

O'Dell was nodding. He knew Tony Jacobs; he was one of the best mechanics in the plant.

"While you're going ahead with painting and other things," Roney went on, "management is going to have a market survey run. They want to be sure the department has a future. They want to know we'll still be selling tubes two years from now, *before* they spend too much dough down here."

"Makes sense."

"Right. I wish I had thought of it. It tells us something we should know. It also tells the men that the department's future is a subject of burning interest with all of us. They'll realize that their jobs aren't absolutely guaranteed now and forever. If the results of the survey are positive, that will tell the men that *they* have some control over their own futures. If they can produce, they can help us capture some of that market out there."

"Want me to tell the men about the survey?"

"You're the logical one. But do it face to face, with groups of your men."

The day after O'Dell had made his announcement, per-man production rose by a little more than 25 tubes per shift. It wasn't much, but it signaled the first breakthrough. O'Dell called Roney when he had all the figures in hand, relating the news with elation.

"It's a start," Roney said. "Keep it up. But remember, they're probably still working in unison. Someone gave the signal and everyone could turn out about 25 more a day. When you've got no such control at all, then your battle is completely won."

THE TALLY SHEET

O'Dell began to keep a record of what he was doing, where the department stood. He began to see slow, steady improvement. The department got its new coat of paint and Tony, the maintenance man, went to work. By agreement with the stewards, he worked on the worst machines first.

Other action came rapidly. A suction vent was installed in the high ceiling over the lines of machines to draw off fumes and smoke and eject them outside. Safety innovations were attempted, including a shower next to the acid bath in the dipping room. The shower was to be used in an emergency— for example, if a man should be splashed with acid. As he worked on the machines, Tony made numerous changes resulting in greater safety for the operators.

Eleven weeks after the Berlin Wall had been put up, the word came down: The market survey showed that the company's tubes would have a good, steady market for the near future and perhaps well on into the coming years. Roney and O'Dell talked about it.

"Now you may be on the trail of the devil—the production restriction," Roney said. "You've already come a long way, your production is up 20 percent, and I think we may be seeing the light at the end of the tunnel."

"Want to know my timetable for the next few months?"

"Sure do."

"I've been keeping a tally sheet on everything we've been doing. We're really getting down into the nitty-gritty on the men's basic gripes. So here's what I'd like to do. First, move Kennelley to the day shift and transfer Piatek to another department. We'd replace Kennelley on the third shift with Simmonds from ovens. Second, I'd like to see us get started on negotiations on the production bonus. That's going to be a hassle that'll take months. I have a feeling, from what I hear from the stewards, that they're both ready to talk and ready to listen to reason.

"Third, I'd like to replace Malvern on the second shift with some guy who won't be so hardheaded about his people. This item may drop: Malvern may come around if we can get a good man on the third shift. Malvern would really be the last of the hardheads at that point.

"Fourth, if everything else works, I'd like to tear out the Berlin Wall."

Roney said, "You're a genius. You want to do all these things after announcing the results of the market survey, I presume."

"Yes, that has to be done right away. But I'd like to see

you do it. It would give the thing more weight, more authority. Remember your bull-board note that started all this?"

"I'll do it."

PSYCHOLOGICAL BOMBSHELL

As analyzed by O'Dell, Roney's report on the market survey proved to be a psychological bombshell. It represented a new departure in company honesty; it placed on the tubemakers the responsibility for continued opposition to the company's goals. Otherwise, the struggle to end the production restriction might have gone on much longer. Once the report had been delivered, men whose livelihoods depended on the continued operation of the department began to reconsider their loyalties. Whether these loyalties should be oriented more to the group than to the company became the burning, if unspoken, question.

Most significantly, the report on the survey (see Exhibit 3-4) was *believed*. O'Dell's communications program had leveled the ground for that. He had told the truth all along; he had promised no more than he could deliver. He had built credibility, and now the company could benefit.

Within a week after Roney's report, Gallarneau, the chief steward, stopped in O'Dell's office, a glassed-in section next to the room housing the foremen's desk.

"We're wondering what the company would think about renegotiating the bonus system," Gallarneau said. "Really, I guess, we're wondering what *you* would think."

"This is a coincidence, Tom. I've been asking myself what you guys might think on the same subject. You got a few minutes to talk about it? You need someone else in here?"

"No. The men know you're not going to bull them. So do our officers. I'll just report back."

The two men talked at length. A *modus operandi* was

3-4. Excerpts from Roney's talk on the tube department market survey.

We have the report on our Tube Department market survey from the Carter Company. We just got it yesterday, and I wanted to get the word on it to you as quickly as possible. That's why we called you in here.

The report is basically favorable. The market for our tubes is there. But as the report points out, we've got to find ways to penetrate it. Those ways won't be found outside the building. They won't be found outside the department. They'll be found right here, by you men and your department management, or not at all. I'm confident that by working together we can find the answers we want.

There are four principal points to make about this survey.

First, the market for the type of tubes we produce will continue—will endure for the foreseeable future. Some new uses have been found for these tubes, including insulation applications for underground wiring. Other new uses may appear.

3-4 (Cont.)

Second, the chances that the market could be further penetrated by us, at today's rate of production, with all that means in terms of labor costs, are slim. We are pricing ourselves out of the market.

Third, there's a clear danger that our company might lose some of its share of the market—about 18 percent right now—unless production and labor costs can be reduced. Other manufacturers are finding cheaper ways to do it. It's that simple.

Fourth, and this is my own comment, our tube operation is marginal at best right now. But a breakthrough on per-tube costs could change all that.

Our production has started to go up and I want to congratulate you men on that. It's your effort that produces that result. We are going to continue to do all we can and we hope you will too.

developed. Gallarneau agreed to O'Dell's suggestion that Kennelley be given the job of representing the company in the discussions. He would be accompanied by a representative of the plant's industrial relations department. A written agreement, replacing the years-old one in effect, would be the target of the talks. Any new agreement would be incorporated later into the union contract.

After Roney's talk, production of tubes per man per shift rose to 1,100. During the negotiations, it rose to nearly 1,200. Even with Piatek gone and Kennelley running the day shift, the third shift continued to post the best record for about three months. Then the day shift started moving ahead. The output per machine began to vary substantially from day to day, an indication that the men were assuming, or being given, the right to produce to their own capacities.

Malvern survived, but it required a major transformation on his part. O'Dell encouraged the change; he himself had been a captive of that old bull-of-the-woods manner of thinking not too long ago, and he could sympathize with Malvern's dilemma.

THE WALL COMES TUMBLING DOWN

The bonus system was an incredible construct. It established a sliding scale for computation of the bonus per individual operator. With a production level of about 950 tubes per shift, an operator reached the optimum per-tube bonus pay-off; from that point on, the payoff slid downward. The system had been established 16 years earlier and the group production limitation had endured approximately as long.

"They were working against their own best interests," Roney said. "Now their whole orientation is changing. You've raised their sights. They have some perspective on where they stand and where they can go. They don't interpret every single thing that happens in the department in terms of their war against the company."

"Over the years, I guess—and I'm not throwing any rocks because I was part of this myself—the bonus system question became obscured. It was at the core of the department's problems, but it wasn't the first thing they mentioned to me in my gripe sessions. It wasn't the first thing anyone thought of. When you thought of problems down here, you thought of production if you were in management. You thought of the mess the place was in if you were a worker. Management couldn't spend any money to fix the place up and get the machines running right because the department was unprofitable. The tubemakers weren't about to increase production because of all the bitches they had."

"Exactly. You've learned something. For one thing, you've learned the answer you give when someone asks you why you're trying to make these guys happy."

O'Dell smiled. "I was asked that at the beginning. I wasn't sure of the answer. Now I am. If producing a satisfying working climate is part of making money, I'm all for it."

"Join my club. What's your timetable now?"

"Well, we've been at this for eleven months. We're on the verge of getting a final agreement on a new bonus system. As soon as we have it, or maybe a few days later, I'm going to tear down the Berlin Wall."

"You've worked this out with the people in ovens?"

O'Dell nodded.

"You're making money now. The variations in daily production from machine to machine tell me your guys are working on their own. You could get my approval on anything."

O'Dell stayed with his timetable. Daily shift production per machine had reached 1,400 and the new bonus agreement had been in effect for a week when he called in the day and afternoon stewards and the day and afternoon foremen. The shifts were changing; a line of men stood at the time clock with their cards in their hands, waiting to punch out. By custom established years ago, they could wash up and hit the clock a couple of minutes before punch-out time.

O'Dell made it short. "I just wanted to let you guys know that we're tearing out the wall," he said. "We should have it down in a couple of days, as soon as we can get the masons in to work on it."

Gallarneau had begun to grin. "No restrictions on use of the aisle? The men can use the vending machines in ovens?"

"Certainly. We'll just appreciate it if they'll make an effort to keep that area clean. That'll keep the ovens people off my back."

"I don't think you have a thing to worry about."

The stewards went out. Gallarneau spoke a few words to the men standing in line. Some of them had started to punch out. As the word went down the line, a cheer went up.

O'Dell, talking to Malvern and Kennelley behind the glass wall of the office, heard the cheer and looked out. The men in line were waving wildly.

"Some things you don't have to announce in a group meeting or on a bull board," he said. He waved back to the men in line, laughing.

4

Women's Lib, Men's Revolt

WALTER DAVIES, PERSONNEL OFFICER for the Belle Isle Plastics Corporation, looked at the petition again. It was headed PLEASE DON'T RUSH INTO THIS WOMEN'S LIB BUSINESS! It indicated, in roundabout but explosive terms, that the 28 men in the Extrusion department were threatening to walk out if the 32 women in the same department were granted rights and opportunities for advancement equal to those of the men.

The 28 men who had signed the petition held in their collective hands the key to the plant's continued operation. Close Extrusion and you soon had to close Shipping and then Printing and Conversion.

Yet the women had a strong case. As packers they came into the plant; as packers they left it unless they transferred to another department. The wage range along which they could be advanced ran from $2.10 to $2.40 an hour, and nearly all of them made it to the top rate within a year. The skill demands left little to be learned after a month or two. Essentially the job consisted in stuffing plastic bags in quantities of three to a dozen into larger plastic bags.

So there it was: 32 women in an Extrusion force of 60 persons. Twenty-eight men in "A" and "B" operator jobs. The women angry for equal treatment—an equal opportunity to take and perform the A and B operator work. The men up in arms because they feared the women were going to take over their jobs, get them thrown out on the street, work for less money within the A and B operator scales.

And today Anna Secondari, main spokeswoman for the women's rights group, had gotten into a loud argument with Miner Jackson, an operator without peer. The subject, inevitably: the approaching equalization of the sexes in Extrusion. In minutes, Davies would face both of them, by request of Axel Warner, president of this far-flung offshoot, by merger, of the conglomerate RJB Corporation.

The pair had agreed to meet in Davies' office immediately following the shift change. That meant they would come in on their own time, at their own request. *That* showed they meant business.

Davies, a thorough man used to headaches, had begun his own investigation of the problem. He knew the law, in particular the law as it applied in his middle western state to the treatment of women in manufacturing industries. He knew too that the state department of labor had given a very mealy-mouthed answer when asked about the law providing that women in industry could not lift more than 35 pounds.

"The law about the weight restriction *is* on the books," a labor man had said,"but we don't dare enforce it. Federal guidelines on equality of the sexes take precedence."

The tune ran similarly for other laws. Could women start a shift between 1 A.M. and 6 A.M.? Could women drive fork trucks? Could women work as the Extrusion operators did, taking no formal breaks and no specified lunch periods, but eating and taking their coffee on the fly? Yes, today they could.

This would be a real migraine. Davies felt older and dumber as he pondered what he would say to Anna and Miner and what he would recommend to Mr. Warner later. The question was charged with emotion.

COMMITMENT ON PRINCIPLE

The facts could be isolated easily. Anna had gone to Mr. Warner and complained. She had not gone over anyone's head with malicious intent; she simply believed in going to the top, especially where the top, as here, held out a standing invitation: "My door is always open." The Secondari–Warner conversation could be charted in retrospect:

Monday

"Mr. Warner, the women in Extrusion are mad furious. They'd like to see the A and B operator jobs opened up to them."

"You—and they—know what you face if you take these jobs?"

"Of course. I not only know, I've done that work in the past, when I was on the second shift."

"OK, we'll check it out. Give us two weeks then we'll get back to you. We're going to have to check with the state department of labor, primarily, on the laws we originally had to abide by. You know, the laws on lifting, breaks, lunches, and so on. Then if we're clear, we'll put an equalization program into effect."

Mr. Warner had promised an answer and, virtually, an equalization program. Triumphantly, Anna aired the news around the department. Some of the men grumbled. Miner Jackson went to Davies to register a complaint for the men. Davies had remained noncommittal, saying the investigation with the labor department was still under way. Jackson had avoided threats, but from his tone it appeared that some of the operators were thinking of seeking transfers, quitting, or going on strike.

Tom Vanderbusch, manager of the Extrusion department, saw his smoothly operating team breaking up over what he considered a flimsy issue. The status quo had served well, he maintained; why not keep it? And patiently Davies explained and reexplained that a principle was involved: Women had to have rights and opportunities on the job equal to those of men.

Duties too? Work capacity too? Adaptability to a different schedule? It was Vanderbusch who asked the questions. He had seen Jackson running like a monkey up the ladder leading to the high superstructure of an extruder, and could not visualize a woman doing that.

CONFRONTATION AND INVESTIGATION

Vanderbusch came in a few minutes before Anna and Miner arrived. Davies was glad; he needed a chance to talk to Van before confronting the two workers.

Thursday

"What did you find out?" Vanderbusch asked.

"We're committed pretty tightly to equal opportunity, not only in hiring, but in promoting and other ways. We have what I'd have to call a tacit OK from the labor people to go ahead and open up the operator jobs. So we'll be going ahead."

Van shook his head. "I don't know. Are you sure Anna is speaking for all the women?"

"Impossible. We know that. But if only one woman asks for the chance to do the job, we'd still have to listen to her. Today you've got no choice. The federal antidiscrimination laws and the whole women's lib climate force you to that conclusion."

"What if the men go out?"

"We've got to find a way to minimize the chance. I think you and I can do it, especially if we can just listen today. I want these two to talk it out of their systems and see if we can't get to something constructive."

"I'll listen. But are you indicating that you're not just going to announce it tomorrow and let it go at that?"

"I mean just that. We've got to protect the department's operating effectiveness as much as we can. We're days away from an announcement."

Vanderbusch seemed to breathe more easily.

TO SKIN A CAT

Davies understood clearly that there were many ways to skin this cat. One plastics extrusion company faced with a similar problem had called in a consultant, an expert in systems, and obtained a learned opinion to the effect that equalization under the conditions existing in the plant was impracticable. The company's management had publicized—flaunted—the report and done no more. That company's personnel man glowed with self-adulation as he related how management, at his suggestion, had passed the buck to the consultant firm.

In another case a company management had simply done nothing. The order had been passed down by word of mouth: "Temporize until it blows over." To all appearances it had blown over, but the company was struggling to move productivity above a bare survival level.

A third company had tried giving women equal rights, found that it "didn't work," and discontinued the policy without fanfare. Women were once again hired for jobs such as packing, and were kept on those jobs. Men remained in all operator jobs. Men could move on to leadman positions, women could not. Men were not hired for packing jobs; that was "women's work."

But in the 1970s there could be no "women's work," Davies reasoned. Beyond that, a principle, or set of principles, had to underlie your decisions, and these had to take into account both human nature and the new conditions governing the relations of men and women in industry. You could no longer fly through these storms by the seat of your pants; pure pragmatism on management's part had led hundreds of companies to unionism, to slowdowns, to strikes, to walkouts.

Principle 1, if Davies had cared to formulate it, would have specified that women had to have equal rights on the job, come what might.

Principle 2 would represent a corollary to No. 1: that the men, in their turn, had to be protected, not prejudiced by what you did for the women.

Principle 3 summed up a belief of Davies. He felt strongly that people in general were reasonable, could see problems the company's way if given the opportunity, and would even make concessions if necessary to make possible an equitable solution, *if* the company honestly sought one.

Principle 4 related to management decision making. Most simply, it indicated that some problems were more complex than others and required deeper study. In all cases, however, a solution was possible given goodwill and an honest search.

Principle 5 required that the people affected be brought into consideration of the problem to the greatest extent possible.

Miner Jackson, the man who could close down this plant simply by going back and telling the other operators that the company was being unreasonable and would not listen to the men's side, had come into Davies' office. Anna followed him a minute later. They sat there, tense in each other's presence: the living, breathing representatives of opposing ways of thought. Much of what they said initially sounded like an extension of their argument earlier in the day. Davies and Vanderbusch listened.

Thursday

"I think she's just stirring up the women," said Miner. He had a sleepy, unkempt look that gave no suggestion of his skill and attentiveness on the job. His hair hung too long, though not dangerously long.

"The women have been talking about this for months," Anna said. "And he knows it. He's heard them. We just think the women work harder than the men and should have the chance to prove they can do any job."

"Work harder?" Miner waxed caustic. "What bull! It might look like they work harder—they have to pack off the machine. But do they know what we're doing half the time when we seem to be standing there? We're making sure that film is coming off right."

"He's right—" Vanderbusch began, but Davies glanced at him and he stopped.

"The men should just try a three-pack all day," Anna said. "They'd find out what work is. Anyway, that's not the point. We want to be able to make what the men make. Some of us have been on this job for four and five years. We're stuck at $2.40."

"They knew what they were getting into when they took the job," Miner said. "Now they're bitching. After they get into the operators' jobs, they'll want to be foremen. Then plant manager. Then president."

"Why NOT?" Anna almost yelled. Davies wanted to say something but did not.

TALKING THROUGH

Gradually, the meeting quieted down. Anna and Miner were clearly running out of recriminations. Now, Davies thought, we can turn to constructive approaches. Quietly, he sketched what he had found, what other companies in the area were doing, what the federal government was asking, what the state labor department had indicated obliquely. There was only one conclusion: Total dedication to sex equality on the job had to be the rule in the context of the mid-1970s. He wanted all this to get out in the department, and it most surely would.

Thursday

Miner spoke as quietly now as Davies had. "When I came here, I started on the third shift," he said. "I waited a year and a half to get on the second and another year to get on the first. That's one thing. You remember, Wally, we decided a long time ago to hire for the third shift and move guys up on the basis of seniority. When a guy came who could only work the first or second shift, he'd get a job only if no one with seniority wanted to move.

"There's another thing. We're working eight hours straight through. We're getting no coffee break, no lunch. We eat on the fly. If the women want to become B and A operators, they should know that they'll be working under that system.

"One more point. We have to lift any box that comes along. No matter how heavy it is, we lift it. Some of us have to drive fork trucks. We have to be able to repair breakdowns, and fast, those of us who're A operators.

"If they can go into it on that basis, they're welcome. I think some of them have been dreaming a little, figuring if they hollered they'd move right up to A operator and stay on packing. That can't happen. They should be B operators first and then work up, same as everybody else."

Anna had listened in silence. "I know all that," she said. "I've worked as a B operator. I've climbed the ladder, done everything Miner said. I can tell him some things I figure we'll have to do that he didn't mention. If the operators' jobs are opened up, we'd have to dress so we can handle them—slacks only, or jeans, so you can climb.

"We'd have to stay on the B operator job as long as a man, learning it. But the men get automatic raises on that job, and a woman would have to, too."

Davies had been making notes. He finished writing in silence. Looking up, he saw Anna and Miner watching him intently. He smiled; they did, too. He asked them if they had any more points he should consider and when they said no, he promised to get back to them very soon.

BREAKING GROUND

Davies had tried unsuccessfully to isolate the root causes of Miner's point of view. Davies had seen, and smiled at, the quote from Leviticus:

"The following scale shall apply: If it is a male from 20 to 60 years of age, the equivalent is 50 shekels of silver by the sanctuary weight; if it is a female, the equivalent is 30 shekels."

Knowing that discrimination on the job went back to biblical times still didn't tell you *why*, not when you considered women like Anna Secondari. Was it

—that women are less attached to their jobs, are more inclined to change from one to another, and in any case only regard a job as a stepping-stone to marriage? At 46, Anna was going nowhere else, only as high as she could climb in the Belle Isle plant.

—that women are weaker physically, or less agile, or less able to bear up under the stress of industrial employment? Anna, wiry, of middle height and strong, could probably do almost as much physically as the average male operator.

—that there are widely differing views of the typical

female role, with men and some women tending to hold that a woman belongs in and should stay in "her place"—the home? Anna supported an aging mother; she owned her home, but to continue to stay in it she had to work outside it. She made regular mortgage payments.

—that women invest less of themselves in a job, take fewer courses, undergo fewer apprenticeships and so on? Anna had never, to Davies' knowledge, taken any outside courses—to what end, when she worked as a packer? But if she were asked to, he knew, she would.

—that women at Belle Isle had poorer attendance records on the average than men and thus are viewed as less job-centered? Anna never missed a day.

The theory had been advanced that the Industrial Revolution had brought about the partial emancipation of women and that, as with the Negro problem, most men accepted as self-evident the concept that women had inferior endowments in most of those respects that carry prestige and power in society. Woman had "her place."

Davies asked himself how he felt about equality of the sexes on the job. He had to face the question personally before he could investigate it honestly. He reviewed what he had read and studied. A niggling sense that the world had gone topsy-turvy, that the whole women's lib question was stealing from woman's essential dignity, not to mention her femininity, clung in his mind. He had to admit it: He was a traditionalist in this regard.

Prejudice of any kind would destroy him here. He would end up giving the Old Man the poorest advice, the kind that is based on emotion or mental hangup. He backtracked, remembering the rules of identifying and getting rid of blocks and filters:

1. Make a deliberate effort to ascertain what words or concepts upset you or arouse resistance. [Women's lib?]

2. Analyze the words and concepts. Ask how they were acquired as part of your mental and emotional baggage and whether you have made any effort to see all sides of a concept, idea, or situation. Ask, too, whether the situations behind the words or concepts have changed so that built-in reactions are no longer justified.

3. Rationalize the impact that the guilty words and concepts have on you. Discuss them freely with others.*

Davies wrote a memo to his department managers. He stood on good terms with them; he spent time with them, toured their departments frequently. He came to their aid on the run when called, and they often called him. His memo (see Exhibit 4-1) set forth the challenge to the plant—to Davies himself and the plant—without suggesting in detail how it would be met.

Davies was breaking ground. He thought he could purge his mind of bias on female equality in industry, but he had to make sure.

MOVEMENT TOWARD CONSENSUS

They sat there in Davies' office, five of them: Byrd, Jenkins, Rountree, Ellison, and, of course, Vanderbusch.

They came prepared. They had considered in depth the possibility that a new plant policy might be in the making. They asked pertinent questions:

□ Would women be eligible for leadman jobs, foreman jobs? "Yes," Davies answered. "But 'eligible' might or might not mean qualified."

*Ralph G. Nichols and Leonard A. Stevens, *Are You Listening?* (New York: McGraw-Hill Book Co., 1957), pp. 101-102.

4-1. Davies' memo on equal job rights.

MEMORANDUM

TO: All Department Managers

SUBJECT: Equal Job Rights

Mr. Warner has asked me to investigate the possibility that female employees of our plant might be granted equal job rights with male employees. In this instance, "equal rights" would probably mean hiring on an equal basis for all jobs, granting female employees the right to hold any entry-level job in the plant, allowing female employees to qualify for and apply for higher-rated jobs, including "A" and "B" operator jobs in Extrusion, and even opening up foreman jobs for qualified female employees.

I'd appreciate it if you would be in my office at 9:00 A.M. tomorrow to go over some of the aspects of this problem. Please come prepared to discuss ramifications in the areas of pay scales, advancement, job specifications and qualification, general morale, and operating effectiveness as all these would apply in your departments. Let me know if you won't be able to make it.

Walter Davies
Personnel Manager

□ Would women require special treatment of any kind? "No," Davies noted. "Equality is equality. We cannot hand the men any discrimination in reverse."

□ Do the wage scales change in any way? Will we still hire packers at $2.10 and table workers in Conversion at $2.00? Will we continue hiring only women for these jobs? "No to the first question, yes to the second and third," Davies said. "Men have—" and he stopped himself.

"I almost said men have shown little aptitude for the packing and table work," Davies said. "I'm thinking old-fashioned. And now I'm going to reverse myself. We will keep an open mind on hiring for the packing and table worker jobs. Some men may be suited to those jobs; some may want a job at *any* wage, just to be working."

"What do you do when a woman asks for a job as a setup man, or woman?" asked Rountree.

"Give her a fair shot at it, same as if she were a man. We either go into a total equality policy or we retain the status quo. We're basically committed to going into it by one technique or another."

Rountree pursued: "Won't we need some kind of standards to apply where setup or supervisory jobs are concerned? Job descriptions or whatever?"

"You mean more formal job descriptions. Yes, we probably will. I'll take care of that." Davies made a note.

"Would equalization include shipping and receiving?" This from Ellison, Shipping/Receiving department manager.

"We have to—no choice there. We can't have it in one department and not in another. But I think in your case it will prove to be academic. We *can* hire men for some jobs, and yours will be some of them. Women *do* have to be able to do the work physically. And I doubt that any woman will apply for a transfer to your department."

"Don't be too sure," Ellison said.

INVESTIGATING IS ANNOUNCING

Davies had to recognize a fact: In investigating, questioning, obtaining opinions pro and con, he was all but announcing that the company would introduce a new policy.

He had that in mind as he talked with his 17 foremen about what lay ahead. They reacted, as he would have expected, in more partisan fashion than the department managers. In essence, they saw the same threat as that enunciated by Miner Jackson. The men, they contended, would walk out, or seek transfers, or leave the company.

They also noted a key point. The women, they said, might try to work into A and B operator jobs, but none would last. What the women were really seeking was parity of pay between the packer and B operator jobs, a range from $2.30 to $2.60 per hour, with no loss of privilege such as scheduled breaktimes and scheduled lunch periods. But Davies insisted that Mr. Warner would not accept that kind of buyoff; the policy, if installed, would have to be an honest one with genuine meaning in the plant's life. Wage scales, for the time being, would remain where they were. A general increase had become effective only four months earlier, in any case. Another could not be expected for eight months, in accordance with the plant's general practice. And finally, packing could not under any circumstances be rated on a par with the operators' jobs—the skill demands were not comparable.

To leave no stone unturned, Davies talked finally with a group of men from the Extrusion department's day shift. He posed a single question: Is there a way in which we can install an equal opportunity policy change without disrupting operations? Miner Jackson was not present.

Monday

Tom North spoke for the group. A huge, heavy-set man, he never hesitated to air his views on any subject. "Wally," he said, "this is a lot of bunk. They're just trying to pressure you. None of these damn women will really take a B operator's job if it's offered to them."

"I don't know. Anyone else feel the same way?" Davies held back deliberately; *they* had to talk it through.

Tom persisted. "There's not a guy in the department who thinks a broad could do that job. A lot of them are saying they'll get out if a woman is put in. Why don't you just pay the women for their lunch period? That's all they want, isn't it?"

"I doubt that I could get the Old Man's OK on that. It might be a possible way out, though. You can see what would happen. If the women get a paid lunch period, the men would have to get something too."

"Why not? This eating on the fly's no fun. If we could get a lunch break and get paid for it, same as they want, we'd feel a lot better."

Heads were nodding. The conversation had taken on some of the earmarks of a bargaining session. Davies said: "And if the Old Man said no? If we have to stay with the system we've been using for years? I've got to check all the angles."

Arthur Jellinek spoke up. "You'd have to find a way to prove to the operators that the women wouldn't be taking over their job," he said. "Also, I think a lot of guys figure if they're on a job for women they don't want it. You know, a matter of pride."

"One thing we couldn't do," Davies said, "is even suggest that a man now on the job would lose out—you know, have to give up his job so a woman could have it. Women would only have a chance at the operators' jobs if there were a vacancy and if they could prove they could do the work. Also, I don't see any chance we'd be suggesting that this job had suddenly become women's work, no more than allowing women to become doctors makes doctoring women's work.   It's everybody's work, everybody's who can qualify."

Others began to contribute. "You'd have to fix up the ladders on those machines. They're dangerous."

"Yeah—and make sure no one could get a shock on No. 3."

"You'd have to start cleaning up the entire department. It's a mess, and that makes it hazardous. We're used to it, but the women—"

"If we could get one break a day—10 or 15 minutes—then you'd be helping us *and* the women. They're not going to stay on that job without breaks or lunch periods."

WHAT'S IN IT FOR ME?

The word had now gone out; a change was probably coming. Beyond that, Davies thought he had found a key: Give the men—and any women who might take A or B operators' jobs—something concrete simultaneously with announcement of the new policy, or just before announcing it. The men, seeing the women in effect bringing in a basic improvement, would be happier with the new dispensation.

Would Mr. Warner accept that kind of political approach? Time would tell.

Davies pondered the problem from several angles. He had to get recommendations to Mr. Warner now, and fast. But he had to understand what he himself was doing.

A basic rule of communication held here: "What's in it for me?" Essentially, that was what the men were asking. If you could show them in action that the newly opened opportunities for women would be accompanied or preceded by a favorable change for the men, they would be more amenable to the idea.

How to overcome or eliminate the suggestion that the new

policy, if installed, would turn a man's job into a woman's?

Deny that the operator's jobs had ever been men's jobs? No way. The men knew better, or thought they knew better. Here, thinking so made it so. The wage differential between the packers and operators which had always been in effect, supported the men's convictions.

Pass over the question. Ignore it and hope the men would come around? Possibly. But not likely. That petition put them on record.

Slowly, subtly indoctrinate the men in the belief that an operator's job is no more the province of men exclusively than medicine is? Again, possible.

Covering all bases, Davies spoke to a group of five packers. Anna was not among them. Davies found the women much less enthusiastic over the prospect of receiving equal access to operators' jobs than he had expected, much less enthusiastic than he would have judged from what Anna had said. He also found them full of feminine paradox. "If we got the right to apply for a B operator's job, and one of us got that job, would she lose her morning break and lunch period?" (Yes, same as the men.) "I don't know how the men go through a whole day without a break for food. I'd be happy with packing if we could get paid for the lunch period." (Impossible, Mr. Warner wouldn't consider it at this time. We'd also have to pay the men for a lunch period that they don't and can't take.) "If you did that for the men, you'd have to pay us for the lunch period and allow us to eat lunch or skip it."

When the women had gone, Davies checked his notes. He felt he had reached the moment of truth. He restudied the petition from the male operators in Extrusion. They had certainly not closed the door on the various options open to the company. Basically, they had only issued a warning. He began to write rapidly. He felt he had already listened his way through most of the problem.

THE PLAN

In the next few days Davies talked to another group of male operators and another group of packers. In the meantime he gave his recommendations to Mr. Warner. They had four main points of focus:

1. That the A and B operators in Extrusion should be granted, without fanfare and without even a bulletin board or other announcement, the right to eat in the lunchroom. Individuals were not to leave the work stations without permission of their leadmen or foremen. Their jobs had to be covered; lunch breaks could be taken any time between 11 A.M. and 2 P.M. Such breaks would in every case be limited to a maximum of ten minutes.

2. That at the same time a crash fix-up, clean-up program be started in Extrusion.

3. That one week after the start of the above program a plantwide announcement be posted regarding the new policy of equal job eligibility and opportunity for men and women. The announcement (Exhibit 4-2) would be spare, brief, unequivocal, plantwide in application.

4. That a special announcement be posted in Extrusion to explain how the plantwide policy would affect that department (Exhibit 4-3).

Davies discussed the plan at length with Mr. Warner. In particular, the personnel man stressed his belief that the way had already been prepared, and would be prepared further in the next few days, for acceptance of the program. No longer would either the men or the women be going cold into what amounted to a new way of life. Both men and women had already had a chance to consider various ramifications of the proposal. Women had been given the opportunity to see some of the drawbacks and, speaking realistically, the likelihood that more than one or two would seek operators' jobs was slim. Davies had already suggested to the women that other issues could not be discussed in connection with the equalization program; swallowing one elephant at a time would present the company with enough of a challenge. And this constituted recommendation No. 5:

5. That other issues, including that of a paid lunch for women, be held for discussion at a later date, if at all.

Mr. Warner accepted all five recommendations. All were put into effect on the schedule suggested by Davies.

OUT OF EXPERIENCE: KNOWLEDGE

The smoke of controversy cleared quickly. Almost everyone in Extrusion accepted the new formula without reservation. Productivity increased throughout the plant. It increased more in Extrusion than in the other departments, however. The women, granted equal job rights, worked harder at the packers' menial, repetitive tasks.

In the first 90 days after the new policy was announced, only Anna Secondari applied for an operator's job. She got it, held it for two months, and then went back to packing, at her own request. Her back hurt from lifting heavy boxes of packaged bags, she said.

Davies had learned a technique that he applied in situation after situation. What he called the "Anna Secondari Case" had taught him that a general pattern could be followed in any approach to a difficult management problem. He had learned to cleanse his mind of hangups and blocks and to take a consistently positive attitude toward problem solving. In listening, he learned to relax, and to follow an old rule: Listen to what the other or others found it hard to say. He found he could read through words to meanings. Always thorough, he investigated as deeply as the situation demanded, and afterward analyzed the findings coolly. In communicating

4-2. The president's statement.

MEMORANDUM

TO: All Plant Personnel

SUBJECT: Equal Rights and Job Opportunities for Men and Women

Thorough study has convinced us that under today's conditions it is no longer realistic to have jobs for male employees and jobs for women employees. The policy that brought about such a situation was once in line with industry practice. Thus the policy was not meant to discriminate against one group or another; it simply reflected what was done elsewhere. Today, in the light of federal guidelines, social trends, and industrial practices, we feel it is in the best interest of all employees to move toward total equality of the sexes.

Starting at once, our plant will adhere to a policy of nondiscrimination. Hiring, assignment to jobs, advancement and promotion, transfer, and other personnel actions will be undertaken without regard to sex. The policy will apply throughout the plant, in all departments.

It should be stressed that, as in the past, personnel applying for, or under consideration for, other job assignments will be required to prove that they can

4-2 (Cont.)

qualify for those assignments. As in the past, qualification will depend in some cases on training or
prior experience. In other cases it will depend on
performance during a probationary period. All
other established policies, including our seniority
regulations, will continue in force.

We realize that in establishing this policy we are
not solving all our problems. We are also aware
that many fine points will have to be ironed out as
we go along. But with goodwill and honest effort,
we believe, we can work out all difficulties.

                                        Axel Warner
                                        President

4-3. Special announcement on new policy.

Guidelines for Applying New Nondiscrimination Policy

For the information of all personnel, we have prepared some guidelines to help us apply our new policy on nondiscrimination in the Extrusion Department. These guidelines are:

1. Female employees in Extrusion may apply for transfer from the job classification of packer to the job classification of "B" operator.

2. Female employees in Extrusion who have successfully completed six months on the job as "B" operators may apply for advancement to the job classification of "A" operator.

3. Advancement from the job classification of packer to the job classification of "B" operator will not be made automatically, upon application, but only if and when a vacancy occurs.

4. As with male operators, female workers accepting the job of "B" operator would be judged for continuation in the classification on ability to perform all the duties of the "B" operator job.

5. In line with our seniority plan, female employees transferring into the "B" operator classification will be on probation in the new assignment for 90 days, during which period they will be allowed to return to their prior assignments in the department without loss of seniority.

6. Female employees accepting the "B" operator classification will be required to work on the same schedule as that worked by male operators.

7. The same skill, strength, and ability standards will be applied to female employees in "B" or "A" operator assignments as to male employees in the same assignments.

8. Female employees in the packer classification in Extrusion will be given opportunity to apply for "B" operator jobs, where such come open, before such jobs are filled either by men or women transferring from other departments or by male or female new hires.

4-3 (Cont.)

> 9. In line with seniority practices applying in Extrusion, advancement through shifts 3 and 2 to shift 1 will remain the rule; where a vacancy occurs in shift 1 (days), personnel on shift 2 will be given the first opportunity to fill that position, on the basis of individual seniority; personnel on shift 3 would have similar priority of opportunity to accept openings on shift 2.

decisions formed on the basis of these findings, he practiced fairness, remembering that communication is what you do more than what you say.

He began to work with the department managers to convince them that the technique could be applied everywhere, in any problem situation. He had the plant's rising record of productivity as proof that the method works.

5

The Step to Man

I REMEMBER THAT MEETING for two reasons. One, I ran into Jack Wyatt on the way to it and was accorded the snotty remark I was accustomed to getting from that individual. I gave it back in spades, really laid him in the peonies. Two, Old Man Pither blew his top.

A word about me. That morning, as I was putting on my white, button-down shirt, my wife told me the church bazaar had been called off. I was a little miffed; it didn't seem right that a bunch of lousy flu bugs running around infecting people should affect an event of that importance. Then as I was tying my dark blue, narrow-knot, no-design tie, she mentioned that the Brenten Door Company, down the street from us, had announced a new policy about men's hair. No longer would any restrictions of any kind be placed on the men or the women employees regarding hair or dress or anything like that—that was the gist of it.

I snorted. "We" in this case is the Hollowell Division of the RJB Corporation. We have about 600 people turning out precision electronic products, and we saw hair, dress, and that sort of thing as being related to both safety and efficiency. That's what we told ourselves anyway. Our policies in these areas were—well, strict.

BEND OUR MINDS

The meeting opened normally enough. Keith reported, Livingston had his usual say ("We had a pretty good week....").

It was winding down, coming to its usual uneventful end, when the Old Man opened up. He has his own ideas about how organizations should be run, and merging with RJB hasn't changed these a single whit. He believes in weekly meetings, for one thing—on schedule. But he doesn't believe in cant, or sitting on your hands, or a lot of other things that find acceptance in so many organizations.

"I'm going to read you something, gentlemen," the Old Man said. He launched into this piece by a guy named Carl Rogers. A couple of hundred words on how knowledge is advancing so fast we'll be lucky if we keep up with it. A little more on the need for adjusting to change, using creativity, that type of thing. Actually, I didn't pay much attention to what the Old Man was saying, but I got a copy of the book later and read the excerpt:

In a time when knowledge, constructive and destructive, is advancing by the most incredible leaps and bounds into a fantastic atomic age, genuinely creative adaptation seems to represent the only possibility that man can keep abreast of the kaleidoscopic change in the world. With scientific discovery and invention proceeding, we are now told, at a geometric rate of progression, a generally passive and culture-bound people cannot cope with the multiplying issues and problems. Unless individuals, groups, and nations can imagine, construct, and creatively revise new ways of relating to those complex changes, the lights will go out. Unless man can make a new and original adaptation to his environment as rapidly as his science can change the environment, our culture will perish. Not only individual maladjustment and group tensions but international annihilation will be the price we pay for a lack of creativity.*

*Carl R. Rogers, "Toward a Theory of Creativity," *Creativity and Its Cultivation* (New York: Harper & Row, 1959), p. 70.

I've read a lot of stuff about creativity. I even attended a company-sponsored seminar on it once. The day of that meeting I was sort of turned off by mention of it; the meeting had been going fine, I had a hell of a lot to do, and here the boss was going on and on.

Now he was reading something else, and he seemed to be angling it to me as assistant plant manager. I also got a copy of this later.

> Great and important things are happening in an area which does not even have a name yet, which we may call organization theory, or the social psychology of industry perhaps, or the theory of enterprise or business.... An example of high synergy...illustrates the possibility of arranging social institutions, whether in business, in an army or in a university, in such a fashion that the people within the organization are coordinated with each other and are perforce made into colleagues and team-mates rather than into rivals.*

When he was done reading, he paused. "Mean anything to you, gentlemen? No? Well, it means something to me. It means we're going to strike out. As I sit here listening to all these reports on how well we're doing, on how we're communicating so well, on how production has risen in the past month one-tenth of one percent, I'm terrified.

"I'm really terrified. I think we're stagnating. I think we need to do some exploring. You know as well as I do that an organization that rests on its laurels doesn't really stand still. It goes backwards. I refuse to accept that fate.

"Here's what we're going to do. You, PeeJay [my two front initials], will dig into this whole subject of mind training. I don't care what you find—I want facts about this subject. I want them at next week's meeting. Tell us about confron-

*Abraham H. Maslow, "Human Potentialities and the Healthy Society," *Human Potentialities* (St. Louis: Warren H. Green, Inc., 1968), p. 75.

tation group, T-groups, whatever you find. Make it as complete as possible. We're going to try some new things and we've got to do it on the basis of evidence. Bend our minds, PeeJay."

Me? I didn't even have a chance to rebut. The meeting adjourned. I got a lot of static the next few days: sly stuff, sly as an elephant standing on your toes. Wyatt got into the act from his eyrie in the testing lab. "Hear you're hiring out as a swami," he said. I could have kicked him.

ALTERED STATES OF CONSCIOUSNESS

I really got hung up on the subject. I read everything I could find. I read some things I couldn't find. They were quoted in journals, that kind of thing.

At the meeting I got back at the others. "The first thing we've got to do," I told them, "is get twelve copies of a book called *Synectics*—one for each of us—and read it.* It's out in paperback." I waved a copy. "It'll give us all the same frame of reference for looking at the mind to see how it operates."

I took over what we called the show-and-tell board. I hung up a chart showing the various altered states of consciousness (Exhibit 5-1).

I had designed it myself on the basis of some of my reading, in particular a piece by someone named Arnold M. Ludwig.†

"For real understanding of this subject," I noted, being deliberately pedantic, "you've got to get an overall view. As the chart indicates, there are five types of altered states of

*William J. J. Gordon, *Synectics* (New York: Collier Books, Inc., 1968).

†"Altered States of Consciousness," in *Altered States of Consciousness: A Book of Readings* (New York: John Wiley & Sons, Inc., 1969).

5-1. Classification of altered states of consciousness according to the ways in which they are induced.

TYPE	EXAMPLES
I. Produced by reduced outside stimulation or motor activity, or both.	Highway hypnosis, sleep, somnambulism; jet-pilot "breakoff," "temple sleep," "kayak disease," "incubation."
II. Produced by increased or heightened outside stimulation, motor activity, emotion, or a combination of all three.	Brainwashing; intensive "grilling," "healing trance," spirit possession states, orgiastic trance, shamanistic and prophetic trance; ecstasy; mental aberrations associated with rites de passage.
III. Produced by increased alertness or mental involvement.	Guard duty or radar screen trance states; deep mental absorption states; intense mental absorption states; intense mental involvement resulting from listening or watching intently for an extended period.
IV. Produced by decreased alertness or relaxation of critical faculties.	Classical mystic, revelatory, or transcendental states, Zen, Zazen, Yoga, Sufism, satori, samadhi, nirvana; autohypnosis; nostalgic or music trance, daydreaming, drowsiness, brown study, reverie; cosmic consciousness.
V. Produced in the presence of somatophysiological factors.	Hyperglycemia, hypoglycemia; extreme dehydration, narcoleptic or sleep-deprivation states; toxic deliria from fever; drunkenness; pharmacologically induced states resulting from narcotic, sedative, stimulant, or psychedelic drugs.

Adapted from Arnold M. Ludwig, "Altered States of Consciousness," in *Altered States of Consciousness*, Charles T. Tart, ed. (New York: John Wiley & Sons, 1969), pp. 13-21. Article originally published in *Archives of General Psychiatry*, Vol. 15, 1966, copyright 1966, 1969 American Medical Association.

consciousness. They're classified by the ways in which the state is induced." I ran through the five types—those brought on by reduced outside stimulation or motor activity, those produced by increased or heightened outside stimulation, and so on. They were lapping it up.

I went on to the characteristics of altered states, producing a new chart (Exhibit 5-2). The same chart laid out the key functions of altered states.

I was enjoying all this by now. With a felt-tip pen I drew a big arrow near the bottom of my second chart. It pointed to the subsection titled "Avenue to New Knowledge or Experience."

"This is where we are, gentlemen, or where we can come in. The possibilities opened up under this particular adaptive function are just about endless. Imagine, for example, how new knowledge or experience can open doors to creativity. Or to plain old communication. Or to getting along with people who may be a little different from ourselves."

I asked for questions. I was thinking of Wyatt.

THE SEARCH FOR MODES

They had questions galore. What about those maladaptive functions? Is there a danger that they can become more prominent, or predominant, than the adaptive ones?

Not if the conditions are controlled, I told them—at least, very little danger. For example, I explained, hypnosis by a quack in a theater might be dangerous, while hypnosis by a trained practitioner under a doctor's supervision might produce far-reaching beneficial effects.

What specific vehicles was I thinking of? I told them: encounter or sensitivity or T-groups, marathons, workshops, and so on, all of them sometimes bundled under the title human relations training.

5-2. General characteristics and functions of altered states of consciousness.

I. *Characteristics*

A. Alterations in thinking
1. Disturbances in concentration, attention, memory, and judgment.
2. Archaic modes of thought, blurring of reality-testing.
3. Blurred distinction between cause and effect.
4. Opposites coexist without conflict.

B. Disturbed time sense
1. Feeling of timelessness.
2. Time is perceived as stopping, slowing, or accelerating.
3. Time is perceived as infinitesimal or infinite.

C. Loss of control
1. Feelings of impotency and helplessness.
2. Feelings of greater control and power
a. Under hypnosis.
b. Identification with power of demagog.
c. Due to mystical and spirit possession.

D. Change in emotional expression
1. Sudden displays of more primitive and intense emotion.
2. Detachment, lack of emotional display or capacity for humor.

E. Body image change
1. Split between body and mind.
2. Sense of depersonalization.
3. Feelings of derealization.
4. Dissolution of boundaries between self and others, the world or universe.

F. Perceptual distortions
1. Superinducing hallucinations, pseudohallucinations, visual imagery, illusions, sense of heightened acuteness of perception.
2. Determined by cultural, group, individual, or physiological factors.
3. Representing wish-fulfillment fantasies, expression of basic fears or conflicts, or simple phenomena like color or geometric patterns.
4. Involving translation of sensory experience: for example, seeing or feeling sounds.

5-2 (Cont.)

G. Change in meaning or significance
   1. Increased meaning attached to experiences, ideas, perceptions.
   2. Loss of awareness of objective "truth" of experience, as in drunkenness.
H. Sense of the ineffable
   1. Inability to communicate essence of experience.
   2. Amnesia (no memory of the experience).
I. Feelings of rejuvenation
J. Hypersuggestibility

II. *Functions of altered states*
A. Maladaptive expressions
   1. Attempts at resolving emotional conflict.
   2. Defensive responses to threatening situations that can arouse anxiety.
   3. Breakthrough of forbidden impulses.
   4. Escape from responsibilities and inner tensions.
   5. Symbolic acting out of unconscious conflicts.
   6. Brain lesions.
   7. Inadvertent and potentially dangerous responses to certain stimuli, like highway hypnosis.
B. Adaptive expressions
   1. Healing process is begun.
   2. Avenues to new knowledge or experience are sought.
   3. Social functioning or ability to interrelate is enhanced.

Adapted from Arnold M. Ludwig, "Altered States of Consciousness," in *Altered States of Consciousness*, Charles T. Tart, ed. (New York: John Wiley & Sons, 1969), pp. 13-21. Article originally published in *Archives of General Psychiatry*, Vol. 15, 1966, copyright 1966, 1969 American Medical Association.

Could I spell out the purposes of this type of experience? Certainly: To give the individual a greater awareness of both himself and others, to enable him to "relate"—ever misused word!—to others better and, as noted, to produce greater facility in communication.

They wanted to know why this experience is called an altered state. "Well," I said, "it has apparently been regarded as one, or as engendering one. When you're in a really effective encounter or sensitivity session, from what I've read, you have a sense of the ineffable. You can see that on the second chart here. You're trying to develop further, to add to your—well, sensitivity, perceptions, insights. You're taking a step into your inner space or, as someone said, 'taking the step to man.'* The experience takes you out of yourself."

"Isn't this psychiatry?" someone asked.

"No, not all," I said, "the psychiatrist works with people who are impaired in the ability to meet the problems of life in order to bring them up to normal. These group methods start with normal people and try to build from there."

"Can we apply a cost-benefit analysis to this whole business if we go into it?" Wyatt piped up.

"Thanks, Wyatt," I said dryly. "Glad to see you're gripped by the excitement of discovery."

"How do we do it? Where? When? What hours? Cost?" This from the Old Man himself.

"Haven't gotten into that fully yet, Mr. Pither. Can I report back next week?"

"You not only may, you'd better." He was smiling. "As far as I'm concerned it's all-systems-go on this." As an afterthought, he added, "On a purely voluntary basis, of course."

---

*Willis W. Harman, "The New Copernican Revolution," *Journal of Humanistic Psychology,* Fall 1969, p. 132.

I called around most of that day, wrote letters. This is a big town we're located in; there had to be an institute or school of the type we were looking for, or so I thought. But it wasn't that easy. Four days passed. I had written to an institute in California, another in Cleveland. Testing the water with Mr. Pither, I was given to understand that I should exhaust all local possibilities first.

Then I learned that the local YMCA was sponsoring a weekend encounter group. Prying around, I garnered further information: An Oasis Center offered sessions in human growth development right here in Chicago. I reported my findings, with financial statistics, at the next meeting. I had also learned that a company could sponsor its own encounter sessions employing a hired leader, called a trainer or facilitator, to act as a human catalyst.

When I had finished my second report, the Old Man called for three volunteers to attend the weekend session at the YMCA. This was to be a road test. Brown, Gordon, and I volunteered. Three guinea pigs.

SOON THERE WERE EIGHT

The weekend proved to be a turning point for me. Gordon came out of it with a slightly less enthusiastic endorsement, and Brown couldn't make up his mind. In any case, we found out what encounter is: a frank and honest exchange among equals, interaction with people.

At the start our leader pointed out that he wasn't there to give directions, and wouldn't. He wouldn't schedule events or procedures; if he become an authority figure, he said, he'd be defeating his purpose in being there. *We* had to teach one another, if any teaching was to be done. *We* had to relate, there and then, one to another. Whatever problems might arise had to be the problems of interaction.

I felt twisted, pulled, and yet enthralled. I was told to try to come across to the others honestly, to communicate exactly what I was feeling. I made the effort; that's where the twist came in. When others did the same, and succeeded in doing it honestly, I saw them fighting the same interior battle. It seemed that we had been hiding much, disguising much, *missing* much. As feedback poured out, as the others told me how I came across, I had an opportunity to match my image of myself with the image I projected. They weren't the same.

I came out enlarged. I had not been scared or scarred. I reported that to Mr. Pither and the others when next we gathered for the weekly staff meeting. Gordon bore me out; Brown voiced his doubts. He had received a scare, he said. He felt as if his world had been undermined. He said so.

"Undermining may not hurt anyone," Mr. Pither said thoughtfully when Brown had finished. "It may help us, actually, to learn that the things we depend on, and guide our attitudes and actions by, may be subject to change. It may open our minds."

On the basis of our guinea pigs' reactions, he issued a call to everyone on what we liked to call our management team to attend the Chicago institute sessions, if they so chose. Eight men said they would try it. The others demurred. Jack Wyatt was one of the eight.

THE CONFRONTATION

The sessions were held over a stretch of eight weeks, one night a week. We chose that method from the various ones offered because we had families, other obligations, interests. Also, I felt that as beginners we might be able to assimilate the experience better if we stretched it out, taking it in weekly

doses and absorbing and practicing as we went along whatever new skills might be developed.

A major challenge of the encounter group method, I
found now, is to create an atmosphere of trust. With such an
atmosphere, the participants feel safe in expressing their real
thoughts, attitudes, sensations, *feelings.* That's what distin-
guishes the experience from that of the work a day world, I
believe; it is one distinguishing characteristic, at least. Outside,
a person finds it difficult to expose his flanks. Everyone seems
to be saying, "Always play your role, don't listen to your own
feelings or the other person's feelings. Stay in your box."

The encounter group leader, if he's expert, can move a
group into an atmosphere of trust very quickly. He doesn't
structure the initial session too much, I now realize; but he
does do enough to get the thing off the ground. He may use
different techniques: For example, in our first session the
leader divided the twenty of us—eight of us from Hollowell,
four of us with wives, and eight men and women from other
companies—into groups of four. Membership in any group
came about purely by random selection. It was "You-you-
you-and-you" and there was a group of four.

Each foursome then took an hour or so to allow members
to introduce themselves to one another. Each member of
each group described himself, his hobbies, his work, his
thoughts; as each took his turn, the others were expected to
listen. That phase over, the entire group came together again.

Now we really got into it. This was real. You do move
into an altered state of consciousness in a good session. I'm
convinced of it. You become absorbed. In a poor session, and
they exist, you receive little impact, and little distractions
reach you easily.

The leader touched it off. "You can say anything you
want to say here," he started out. "You can blow your mind,
go crazy, commit verbal suicide, tell your boss he should stop

kicking you, get turned on, get an experience; that experience will change your life, and I hope you'll go ahead and do it. We belong to the same human race and we're trying to learn the same things about ourselves and others.

"I presume you all came of your own free will—or at least you bosses let it look like free will. While you're here you are supposed to be grown-up, responsible, serious. That doesn't mean restrained or withdrawn, understand. It means honest. You don't have to take part actively; we have some people who come to these things and hardly say a word and write back to say the whole experience changed their lives. But it's much more likely to change your life if you can honestly face yourself and what you are while among friends.

"We are friends here."

They began to open up. Tentatively at first, then more enthusiastically. I felt like an old hand; I held back, I think, to keep from seeming to push myself out as an old hand. They talked dreams. Bugs. Fear. Fear of bugs. Neuroses. I was in it now. I thought I had my share of neuroses, and more.

"I have a tendency to feel organizationally cramped," I said. "I hate to have my whole future dependent on the success or failure of one company. But that's the way it is. What choice do you have? I wake up at night sweating, thinking about the guys I've heard of who have been dumped by their companies a week before their rights in the retirement fund became vested. Where's the solution to that feeling?"

They talked, ridiculing, questioning, theorizing: It was an inadequately developed sense of personal security; it traced back to something that we all feel, like fear of death or fear of old age; it had its origins in childhood loss sensations. They made me talk about it more.

The second session, the following week, it happened again, but better. And Wyatt and I met head to head.

The talk had turned to job relationships, as I suppose it had to. That area of our lives lay always near the center of our thoughts. When Wyatt said, "The people in our company think I'm a bum," I knew this would be it for both of us. It made me kind of glad. "They don't like it because I go around pricking their corporate bubbles," he continued. "I believe we all take our jobs seriously—"

I interrupted: "Do you try to make yourself disliked? Do you prick bubbles out of spite? People think you're too negative, not company-minded."

"People do—or *you* do? Which? Which of us is being more constructive at work? You or I? I work as many hours as you, maybe more. I think it does the company good to have bubbles popped."

"That may be why we're here—one reason anyway. But isn't there a way to do it decently, politely? A lot of people walk around you. They see you coming and they step into a washroom and go into a stall."

"Each of us turns someone off. I don't care. I would guess that the Old Man, you, Gordon there, *everyone* has relationship problems. It's just that the higher you get on the ladder, the easier the problems are to hide or live with. You can pull rank or do whatever else is necessary. The rich are eccentric, the poor are crazy. I just can't accept it."

The leader came in: "This could be very constructive. We're trying to see ourselves as others see us. How do others here see Mr. Edwards here?" He indicated me.

"He seems straitlaced," one woman said. "Old-schoolish, you know?"

Gordon said, "You should see him after a three-martini lunch," and everyone laughed. Where some tension had been developing, the air suddenly became lighter. I had been moving to the defensive, I saw. I relaxed.

"The mirror throws back an unfortunate image," I said.

"But aren't we all products of something? And can't we all change?"

They all registered general agreement at that.

BACK AT THE RANCH

That session went on a long time. I became weary while remaining excited, engaged, immersed. I began to feel as if I had known these people all my life, not for x or y years, months, or hours. Did that feeling represent the sense of timelessness that comes with some altered states of consciousness? I believe so. Beyond that, I had no sense of immediate time. I felt as if I hadn't slept for days; actually, I had been up only since 6 A.M.

We went through some emotional high points. One man cried—tears of release and joy, not sadness. He came out of it quickly, smiling. One of the women demonstrated with piercing screams how her children affected her.

At the end, I felt younger. I felt "high." I felt I had gained some new emotional kinship with the entire human race. Nothing could touch me now, it seemed. Or if anyone did reach me with annoyances or problems, it would only be temporary. I could shake it off. I had charged some batteries that would not run down for a long time. I was whole, in a strange new way.

Back at work, I talked with the Old Man, at his request. I gave him my honest opinion: "I like myself better. I have more confidence in myself." I was thinking that I couldn't even have said that to him a year earlier. "I think I'll get along with people better. I think I know people better. I can see them from their points of view. Someone could get mad at me now and I think it would roll off; I wouldn't take it personally."

He was impressed. "The others, or most of them, are telling me the same thing. Not all of them. You're in what I'd call the enthusiastic group. There's another couple who say the experience is helping them, but they're not sure how or how much. One of you says it's a total dud."

"Wyatt?"

"Not Wyatt. He's enthusiastic."

I suddenly realized that Wyatt and I had something in common. In fact, a new awareness was taking shape: He and I were more *alike* than different. But the Old Man was talking.

"This human potentials thing has really impressed me. Our meetings are even getting better, it seems. No one seems to have come out of it with any hard feelings. I'm going to try it myself."

He asked about alternatives to encounter. I listed some: lectures, yoga, Zen, astrology, alpha wave training, behaviorism, dance, others. Since Mr. Pither seemed to want more information, I tried to sum up:

"It seems to me that there can be real advantage for both the individual and the company in this effort," I said. "But I wouldn't force anyone to go. I'd be as selective as possible about the leader—with a good one, you're almost assured of a good session. The encounter can actually become a way to learn, as its proponents claim. I have the feeling that as a way to learn it involves the whole person, not just part—not just the intellectual or the emotional halves."

"I wonder if there are other things we should be doing in addition to encounter or similar projects," the Old Man said.

"Human relations training?" I asked. He nodded. "Well," I said, "can I research it a little?"

He was smiling. "You're the expert. Go ahead."

I was on my way back to my office, just a few yards down the hall from the Old Man's, when someone called my name. It was Wyatt.

"Hi," I said. "You seem to have lived."

"So do you," he said, grinning. "Got time for coffee? I'd like to go over some of the new quality control systems we're considering for that Bronson job." He paused. "By the way, what are you doing in that colored shirt and jazzy cravat?"

"Just thought I'd be in tune with the times," I said, "to match how I feel."

6

White Collar,
Red Neck

"Would you take a note, Miss Hause?"

John Downey, office manager, RJB Corporation, examined the papers on his desk. Miss Hause, his secretary, came in and sat down. Bridging his fingers, Downey dictated.

"Dear Miss Furlong—" Downey thought he heard Miss Hause suck in her breath, but couldn't be sure. He glanced quickly at her; her eyes were fixed on the notebook in her lap. "An examination of our policy manual (initials in caps, Miss Hause, as usual) reveals that you are not entitled to pay for the day of sick leave you took last week. . . ." He continued, adding his regrets and a rationale: "If we didn't follow our policy, we would of course have no policy at all."

Miss Hause left. Downey began making notes on the yellow pad in front of him. Pausing, he looked out the window. From here, he could look across the green lawn that stretched away from the RJB Corporation's Admin Building down to Porter Street. The Admin Building stood alone in this green sea. To the south, if he had had a window on that side, Downey could have seen the stacks of the Calvin Park plant, the biggest of the corporation's local facilities.

Downey was still making notes, working up a report for Martin Gray, vice president of personnel, when Joe Bowerman came in. Bowerman was supervisor of the eight women in

Accounts Payable.   Annoyed, he came straight to the point.
"What did you tell Annie Furlong?" he said. "She just
came in and told me she's resigning effective Friday. I don't
know how I'm going to replace her."

Downey explained, but even to him it sounded uncon-
vincing. "It's policy," he said in conclusion. Bowerman left,
shaking his head.

In the next half hour, two other department supervisors
called to say that they were losing one girl each—resignations.
Bowerman called to say he was losing a second woman from
his department—resignation.   And Al Gerry in Electronic
Data Processing called to tell Downey he had heard that three
of his key men were taking other jobs in the next few weeks.

TERMINAL INTERVIEW A QUATRE

The four women agreed to talk to Downey together. He
wondered what was going on. He felt dragooned, but what
choice did he have? Mr. Gray was putting pressure on him to
"get to the bottom of what's going on in the Admin Building."

What was known to be going on had a number of un-
pleasant facets. Not only had turnover risen steeply in the
past six to twelve months (to 18 percent for the month of
March); there was evidence everywhere of sloppy, negligent
work. Even the switchboard operator, usually personable and
pleasant, had become snappish. Absenteeism was on the up-
swing, theft in the Admin Building had increased, break times
were being observed more and more raggedly, grievances and
complaints to supervisors had multiplied enormously. And
someone had scribbled on the wall of the women's washroom:
"General increase—Calvin Park Plant—5.8 percent! Admin
Building?????????"

The four women arrived together, as if they had met elsewhere and then come to Downey's office in a body. They were cool, businesslike, rigidly contained. In age, they ranged from the late 30s down to about 23. They had been with the company from two to seven years. All four had excellent records.

Mr. Gray had advised Downey to "just listen," and he did. "Apparently we've got to make some changes around here," he said. "You girls could help us, if you want to."

"Why didn't someone do this earlier?" Ann Furlong asked. "Talk to some of us, that is. You might have avoided a lot of problems."

Touché. Downey felt himself bridling a little. But he said quietly: "Is it that important to a lot of people? I'm really seeking information."

All of them spoke. "Yes, it is." "Of course it is." And so on. Then they were talking, organizing their thinking, each reinforcing what another said. Downey made notes on his pad. The meeting lasted two and a half hours; at its end Downey said: "Tell me one more thing—or, rather, two things. A lot of the items you've mentioned could be corrected by this office, right?"

The women nodded.

"Second, if I promised that you'd see a completely new approach here, would you consider staying on?"

The women looked at one another. They had been relaxing; all tensions seemed to have dropped away. "I suppose I would," Ann Furlong said. "Basically, I like it here. It's just—well, that note I got from you the other day is an example. I haven't even been able to find out what the policy on sick leave is, then I got that note. I suppose if you could find a way to stay in touch with people, to get questions answered—"

The others agreed. They would stay and try it.

FOUR PRESSURE AREAS

Downey made an appointment with Mr. Gray for Monday and then spent the weekend analyzing his notes. They seemed to focus on four main problem or pressure areas:

1. "We don't feel like people."
2. "We have too many bosses—we're oversupervised."
3. "You don't even know what job you're supposed to be doing."
4. "The policies that apply to us are both unclear and inhuman."

The women had mentioned other problems, but they seemed somewhat peripheral. Even the question of wages had been mentioned without special emphasis or passion.

Downey listed under each of the four headings some of the comments pertinent to each (see Exhibit 6-1). And he remembered things. As office manager, *he* had called for a "pretty tight ship" as far as the Admin Building employees were concerned. *He* had gone along with the policy, or nonpolicy, of not showing employees the policy manual. *He* had agreed that it should merely be "interpreted" for those seeking information. *He* had accepted the rationale behind that nonpolicy: that invidious comparisons might be made between the policy manual for nonexempt employees—employees "on the clock"—and the union contract at the Calvin Park plant. If the union found out, for example, that Admin Building employees received sick-leave allowances based on longevity, the union would surely ask for the same in the next contract negotiations.

There was more. Downey himself had suggested that no general raises be granted in the Admin Building: "Spread them out over a year," he had said, "give them when the employee is up for his performance review. It's a lot cheaper."

6-1. Sample comments made by Admin Building employees.

"We don't feel like people."

We never get any real news around here—not the big news. If someone has a baby, we may hear about that. . . .There are a lot of things happening in the company that would concern us; sometimes the girl at the switchboard doesn't even hear for days when someone has left the company. . . .Nothing that has to do with us happens on time. The performance reviews are the best example. . . .I've never had a performance review on time. . . .The supervisors, or some of them, seem to think we're a lower order of being. . . .The lunchroom is always crowded when we get to it—with men. A lot of us have to eat in the washroom. . . .No one ever explains new equipment or programs to us. We have to find out for ourselves. . . .People leave here and then they hire someone else at higher pay. . . .

"We have too many bosses—we're oversupervised."

You never know what job to do first, you get so many conflicting orders. . . .You get work from two or three different people all at once—all rush work. Then they sit on your back until you get them all done. . . .I think I'm assigned to Accounts Payable, but I'm always being moved over to Accounts Receivable to help out. They never come over to help *us* out. . . .A lot of people leave because they don't really know who their boss is; they're getting orders from all directions. . . .You can't work for five masters. . . .They check on us all the time—watch when we come in, when we go on break, come back, go to lunch, go to the washroom; it's like a kindergarten. . . .

"You don't even know what job you're supposed to be doing."

We've mentioned this—you don't know what you're supposed to be doing—but somebody should really do something about it.

6-1 (Cont.)

It's nerve-wracking. . . .You'll start something and then be taken off it. . . .I'm supposed to be working as a typist, but I run all the errands in our department. . . .The job classification system is meaningless. Some girls don't even know what classification they're in. . . .They hire for one job and then you never do it. . . .You come in, and they tell you you'll get a raise in 30 days. Then it never comes, and when you go and ask about it, you're told it will come when you get on your regular job. . . .

"The policies that apply to us are both unclear and inhuman."
Is there a way to get all the departments working the same way as far as salary administration, performance reviews, and other things are concerned? People get mad when they find different departments doing things differently. . . .It seems none of the supervisors really knows what he's supposed to be doing in these areas. . . .That sick-leave policy should be changed. People think they have sick leave and then they don't. . . .It's as if they get mad when you get sick, and most people are really sick when they stay out. . . .Leave of absence is just as bad—it doesn't take into consideration that we're human. . . .What is the order of action under the performance review system—appraisal, then a recommendation on a raise, then the raise if any, and then the interview between the employee and the supervisor? . . .Is the two-and-one-half percent raise mandatory for office people—for all of us? If so, someone should look into it because a lot of people didn't get that much. . . .

And now there had appeared a scrawled comment on the wall of the ladies' washroom.

Reading books of theory, Downey found that white collar alienation has roots as deep as emotion, as broad as people's goals and needs in working. The needs roster on a white collar employee would be the same as for a blue collar employee: recognition as an individual, adequate job training, good supervision, acceptance by the group, adequate communication, fair wages and benefits, and so on. But blue collar alienation—what people were calling "blue collar blues"—was more easily explained. His blue collar alone set the plant worker apart. The white collar worker sat closer to his or her boss, dressed like the boss, and normally identified readily with the boss's thinking.

You had to work, actually, to achieve white collar alienation. So said many experts.

THE RECKONING

There were several ways to go, Downey saw. You might raise entry-level wages. But even if that were acceptable to top management, you couldn't raise the wages of one category of employee without raising all categories. Wages didn't even seem to be the focal point of pressure here.

You could train supervisors. You could provide on-the-job training. You could establish a system of rewards to make sure individuals received adequate recognition. You could, possibly, improve working conditions.

Studying his notes again, Downey tried to identify each specific complaint as falling under one or another of the key "employee needs" headings. Some fell under more than one heading; for example, some related both to "adequate communication" and "recognition as an individual." But toting up the results when he was finished, Downey noted with something like shock that 85 percent of the items fell at least once under the heading of communication.

There it was. The evidence said that the major flaws in the Admin Building's "mini-society" were traceable to inadequate communication.

More became apparent. The entire complex of events, operations, policies, relationships, and decisions that made the Admin Building a functional entity had been falsely viewed. Management measured all those things for efficacy almost entirely on the basis of the actual or potential contribution to profits. In so doing, Downey concluded, management had been undermining morale. Nothing was geared to the individual. The individual rebelled by quitting, or staying home more frequently, or turning in poor work, or simply badmouthing management.

Four women had pointed out instances where communication on the part of management had produced negative reactions.

□ A bulletin board memo had explained that the policy on leaves of absence provided for LOA's on an emergency basis only. "Personal reasons" would be inadequate: the sickness of a child, a wife's desire to take a week's vacation at the same time as her husband, similar reasons.

So people lied. They invented emergencies. They produced documents to prove that nonexistent emergencies really existed.

□ An edict from Downey himself had been passed to all 140 workers in the Admin Building. The message, in the form of a payroll stuffer, amounted to a plea/demand that everyone try to improve the quality of his work.

People made more errors than ever before. More typing came in late, more papers were lost or misfiled. Some negligence had the odor of sabotage.

□ Downey had *written* to Miss Furlong instead of discussing the situation with her and giving her an opportunity to tell her side of it. Having received one written communication too many, she quit.

THREE QUESTIONS

Downey listed three questions on whose answers, he believed, rested his future success as office manager in the Admin Building:

1. Could every piece of communication, every action, and every policy help one or more of the Admin Building employees satisfy a need or galaxy of needs that they brought to work as people?

2. Would it be possible, while making the effort so to gear communications, actions, and policies, to gain more and more accurate assessments of individual workers' needs, reactions, and relationships?

3. Would it be possible, as this effort unfolded, to meet basic *management* needs?

Downey thought all three questions could be answered positively. He *had* to find positive answers or, in all likelihood, another job. McGregor's Theory Y would have to provide the guiding force behind management thinking and acting; the needs and interests of the individual worker had to become meshed with the needs and interests of management. Communications had to be broadly based so that the needs of the individual and the group were known clearly and thoroughly.

But what was communication? An informal/formal process of exchanging information? And of those, informal and formal, which was more important?

Was it reading, writing, speaking, listening? Was it only these? Or was it also establishment of a tone, an atmosphere that found sustenance as much in unspoken, unwritten expression as it did in written or spoken words and phrases?

Of the so-called four horsemen of communication—reading, writing, speaking, and listening—which was to be rated as primary? Which helped most to establish tone?

A miracle had occurred. Four women had agreed to give it another try. That taught a lesson: listening, the source and wellspring of the miracle, took precedence over the other three aspects of communication.

Listening established tone. That meant that face-to-face communication was called for to the greatest possible extent. That in turn meant informal communication. That in turn meant people-to-people communication in an atmosphere of receptiveness. That meant knowing your people.

It all came full circle. Downey went through his notes again. He drew up a list of half a dozen things to do (see Exhibit 6-2). If he could obtain the cooperation of top management in getting them done, further problems might be reduced drastically.

A MONDAY BEGINNING

It began on Monday, the Monday following *that* Friday. Downey talked privately with Martin Gray, an intuitively rational man with a leonine head. Gray readily agreed to stand behind Downey's new approach.

"I think you're showing great daring as well as wisdom in taking this new tack," Gray said. "I'll do anything I can to help. It's the new way and I think the right way. In any case, we can't do much worse than we've been doing. But you would be well advised to expect an uphill battle."

Downey agreed, and before leaving obtained Gray's agreement to take part in the program actively. As a starter, Gray would give one of a series of talks for Admin Building employees on a variety of subjects of companywide importance.

6-2. Downey's six-point program.

1. Provide channels for better upward and downward communication.

All the present means of downward communication should be reviewed and revised as required. All the present, very limited number of upward communication methods should be reviewed and then formalized, extended, renewed. Listening on a face-to-face basis has to be incorporated into the upward communication techniques.

2. Locate and deal with grievances or complaints as quickly as possible, employing some established routine or set of practices.

Where grievances fester, trouble of one kind or another is brewing. This applies whether the grievance or complaint is considered "major" or "minor." A formal complaint procedure will be needed.

3. Teach management by any available means to be employee-centered, not job-centered.

More emphasis needs to be placed on encouraging the employee, answering his needs, and showing concern for him as an individual. Less emphasis should be placed on results; the impression should never be given that the employee is another office machine to be operated or pushed around at will.

4. Find ways to make supervision more expert, less based on push and drive, more dependent on leadership.

White collar workers in the Admin Building should be treated as mature adults who know what they have to do, and do it, without continual observation. Supervision should be taken as being more a process of removing irritants than of pushing, hauling, and tugging.

6-2 (Cont.)

5. *Foster greater employee identification with management.*
The specifics of such an effort would await subsequent study and determination; they would have to be adjusted to the opportunities of the moment. Over the long term, the approaches would have to include those listed by Blum: Act on salaries and employee benefits, treat employees as individuals, delegate more authority and responsibility, and so on.[*] But a serious attempt should be made at least to bring employees into management thinking and to standardize policies and procedures for all personnel, from white collar nonexempt employees to officers.

6. *Examine and change personnel policies in general where such examination and revision seem required.*
The whole range of policies and practices, from the conduct of performance reviews to noncommunication of subjects covered by the policy manual and on to training and promotion practices, have to come under scrutiny.

[*]Adapted from Albert A. Blum, *Management and the White Collar Union,* AMA, 1964, p. 51.

Monday afternoon, Downey met with the department supervisors. These "white collar foremen" had rarely met as a group; meetings had not been considered necessary, not even by Downey himself. Now he wanted to change that. He wanted the supervisors' inputs, their ideas, their suggestions. He had to understand them better before he could influence them in the desired directions. He opened simply:

"Gentlemen, as you know we had a crisis here last week. We nearly lost four of our key workers. We settled the problem, at least temporarily. What we'd like to do now is avoid a repetition.

"We have high-level approval to try some new approaches. I'm going to need your help in carrying them out. I hope to be able to sketch some of these new ideas for you in future meetings. But right now I'd like to get your readings of problems in your own bailiwicks that we can help with. We can't attack everything at once. But we hope to get to problems one at a time.

"One thing I want to avoid is to give the impression that anyone is to blame for what happened Friday. If anyone was, I was. But it's water over the dam. I think we can move ahead now with some hard-won knowledge and experience to guide us."

There were questions; there was doubt. Downey as office manager had no direct authority over these men, and had to win their cooperation by tactical means. But many of them were worried and were willing to try anything. Charlie Wright expressed the feelings of the group:

"If four women were ready to leave Friday, so were a lot of others. All it would have taken was a little push. That means there's a mood here that we should try to kill—change would be a better word."

"Mood and morale. They interconnect," Downey said. "I have the feeling that morale is a longer-term thing, more difficult to get at. We have to try to change it for the better. Then their moods will improve. You won't have a lot of people desperate to leave all at once. You'll still have some turnover, but hopefully not on the scale that we've been experiencing."

At the end of the day Downey saw Gray again briefly and reported that he had planted the idea of supervisory training. He had talked in passing with the four women who had planned to leave, indicating to each that he would sit down again with them soon. He also told them he was seeing progress, and was hopeful that it would continue.

MOMENTUM AMID SETBACKS

Painfully slowly, the situation changed. Most of the supervisors gradually became involved, yet two or three missed every weekly meeting that Downey called. It soon became evident that unsolved problems were pretty much localized in the departments of these men.

Downey personally took on the job of clarifying the policy manual for the Admin Building employees. But first he had to obtain permission on an angle of approach: Questions on written policy would be answered in small group meetings; nothing would as yet be put out in writing; the exact wording of responses to questions would be a matter of judgment, and Downey would exercise that judgment. That meant (1) that fear of what the union in the Calvin Park plant might do if it learned certain facts about Admin Building policy was dying hard and (2) that Downey had been handed the responsibility for policy interpretation (and God help him if misunderstandings or problems arose).

He took the responsibility. He was face to face with Max Weber's dictum that a bureaucracy fights hard to preserve the concept of the official secret.

As the small group meetings became part of the fabric of Admin Building practice, people opened up more and more. Some began to come to Downey's office *after* the meetings; these employees had things to say, or ask about, that they had not wanted to mention in front of others.

Sara Christman had such a problem. "I've had two years of college, as you know, Mr. Downey," she said. "I'm wondering whether I might move into a job where I could use that training a little more."

Downey questioned her, then said he would look around. He did not forget; he looked around. He found that Sara's request, reasonable though it was on the surface, probably disguised an ulterior motive: The young woman wanted to get out of Al Gerry's EDP section. Gerry was *the* most recalcitrant of all the supervisors. He had attended no meetings after the first one; he had pooh-poohed Downey's effort; in essence, he represented the conservative opposition. On Downey's success or failure with him might, just possibly, hinge the success or failure of the New Look.

Downey had much to do. He was recasting the Admin Building newsletter, the *AdmiNews,* so that it would reflect employee interests more accurately. He was conducting supervisory training sessions, some of them periods of instruction in the complexities of the policy manual. He was organizing the series of talks by top executives on company affairs. He was dealing personally with literally dozens of individual problems. To the extent that he could, he had launched a war on bombast and "companyese" on bulletin boards and elsewhere. At Gray's request, he had drawn up a list of 20 questions that they called "A Listening IQ Test." Gray had it circulated to all the executives in the Admin Building (see Exhibit 6-3).

Now Downey decided to directly confront the problem represented by Al Gerry.

6-3. Downey's "Listening IQ Test."

1. Do you go into a listening situation, with a subordinate in particular, prepared to change your attitudes or opinions in response to valid comments or suggestions?

2. Do you go into a listening situation prepared to *take action* in response to what you hear, where such appears justified?

3. Do you concentrate while you are listening and attempt to understand not only what is being said but also what lies behind the speaker's words—what he can't say or finds it hard to say?

4. Do you *show* that you are paying attention to what is being said without doodling, reading, making telephone calls, and so on?

5. While listening, do you keep in mind that you are probably listening not merely to one person but also to others, perhaps many others, who share that person's sentiments?

6. Do you understand, in listening, that opinions are facts, right or wrong, correct or incorrect, that the fact that a person holds an opinion is something that must be considered in formulating a response?

7. Are you able to hear someone else out *to the end of what he has to say?*

8. In listening, can you withhold any counterargument or display of disapproval that would terminate the listening exercise prematurely?

9. Can you mentally summarize what has been said by another, while he is speaking or afterward, so as to be sure you have understood it?

10. Do you, by word or gesture, encourage the listener to go on to make sure you get the whole story?

11. Do you examine the evidence a speaker is adducing, with the aim of making sure it really supports any contentions?

6-3 (Cont.)

12. Can you hold your temper even while listening to criticism of a policy or program or attitude in whose genesis you had a hand?

13. Can you empathize with a speaker, no matter who he is, by putting yourself in his shoes, seeing a subject from his point of view?

14. Are you genuinely interested in hearing what others have to say about the organization and its problems and successes?

15. Do you accept emotion and sentiment in the speaker while you are engaged in a listening exercise?

16. Do you strive to use listening to induce creativity—ideas, new inputs—in the other person?

17. Do you listen to all persons, subordinates in particular, equally, without regard to their appearance, background, education, training, speech characteristics, and so on?

18. Do you avoid "tunnel listening"—that form in which the listener accepts only what he wants to hear?

19. Do your subordinates come to you with both their problems and their successes (not only with their successes)?

20. Are you able to just listen and keep silent while another is speaking?

Score: *If you answered "No" to ten questions or more, you're in trouble.*

REACHING THE UNREACHABLE SUPERVISOR

Gerry represented a breed that was alive and well and had membership in most companies. An outstanding technical man, he was also strongly opinionated, sharp-tongued, cynical, hardworking: the archetypical Theory X manager. He saw himself as indispensable. Because turnover was so high in his department, few lasted long enough to learn the department's work and procedures thoroughly and, by default, Gerry *was* almost indispensable.

When Downey indicated in a personal conversation that Sara Christman was eligible for a more intellectually demanding job in Personnel, Gerry snorted: "She just wants to get out of my department."

Two days later Sara was transferred—by order of Gray.

Downey had gone over Gerry's head. The battle lines were drawn. The battle itself took place over the complaint procedure that Downey had installed as a permanent upward communications mode (Exhibit 6-4). The sequence of events, as Downey plotted it later, led straight to a confrontation that had to have long-term fallout.

June 4 Downey's newly drafted complaint procedure goes into effect. It had been passed around to all office supervisors in draft form prior to finalization. The comments of supervisors had been taken into consideration in the final draft. Gerry had not commented at all.

July 10 Gerry instructs Tom Algernon of the EDP section to run a job for Accounting before one for Payroll. Algernon, expert on the 360 computer, runs the jobs in reverse order. Confusion and consternation result when Accounting doesn't have its printouts on time. Gerry then reprimands Algernon.

6-4. Employee complaint procedure.

INTRODUCTION

The following complaint procedure has been established to assure each employee that his problems or complaints about working conditions, treatment on the job, salary, promotions, or other aspects of his employment in the Admin Building will receive full and fair consideration. It is our sincere desire that this formal procedure for the review of complaints will provide an effective means for adjustment of honest differences. To do so, both employees and management must conduct themselves in such a manner as to encourage responsible use of the process.

The complaint procedure does not change some aspects of our life in the Admin Building. Employees will continue to have open and free access through normal channels to the offices of their immediate and higher supervisors, or to their administrative representatives. Such channels should be a court of first resort where problems or complaints arise.

Where normal channels fail to provide satisfactory answers in specific instances, the complaint procedure should be used. But frivolous or spiteful complaints, or uninformed or irresponsible answers from the management side, will undermine the procedure to the detriment of both employee and company.

WHAT IS A GRIEVANCE?

A grievance that could justify use of this procedure is any complaint initiated by an employee that concerns terms or conditions of employment or company policies and actions of management and supervisory personnel that affect an employee's job status.

WHO MAY FILE A COMPLAINT?

Any nonsupervisory employee of the Admin Building may file a complaint under the conditions set forth in this procedure.

6-4 (Cont.)

PROCEDURE

The subject matter of the complaint must first be discussed with the employee's immediate supervisor prior to its submission in writing at Step 1. The employee must wait five days, or until an unsatisfactory answer is received from the immediate supervisor, whichever occurs first, before processing his complaint to Step 1 of the procedure. An employee's immediate supervisor must be informed of the employee's intention to process the complaint further. A complaint must be presented to Step 1 not later than 30 calendar days after the occurrence that gave rise to the complaint.

Step 1. All complaints, excepting those involving layoff or discharge, must be filed with the employee's immediate supervisor on complaint forms available at the Admin Building office manager's office. Complaints involving layoff or discharge will be filed directly with the office manager.

If it is necessary that a conference be held between the employee and his supervisor to adjust the complaint, such a meeting will be held on company time. The supervisor is required to provide the employee with a prompt written answer to any complaint presented. The employee may then accept or reject the answer.

Step 2. The appeal of the complaint into Step 2 of the procedure must contain an explanation of the reasons why the decision of the immediate supervisor is not satisfactory, or must indicate that no answer was forthcoming within five calendar days from the time the complaint was presented. The appeal, to be directed to the office manager of the Admin Building, must also contain a statement by the employee that the supervisor has been informed that the employee intends to process the complaint to Step 2.

The office manager, or a representative of the office manager,

6-4 (Cont.)

will make any investigation considered necessary and will attempt to effect an adjustment of the complaint. The office manager will be required to submit a written answer, setting forth the reasons for his decision on the complaint, within five calendar days after the complaint is received in Step 2.

Step 3. If the office manager or his designated representative is unable to agree upon a mutually satisfactory settlement of the complaint, the employee may appeal his case to the vice president, personnel. Such appeal must be made within five calendar days after the receipt of the Step 2 answer, or if the employee receives no answer from the office manager or his representative within five calendar days. The appeal to Step 3 must contain an explanation of the reasons why the decision of the office manager is not satisfactory to the employee.

The decision of the vice president, personnel, will be considered final unless unusual, important issues are involved in the complaint. In such a case the employee will be notified within five days from presentation that his complaint has been referred to appropriate management officials for additional consideration. A decision will normally be made within 30 days, and the employee will be promptly notified of the decision.

July 15   Algernon files a complaint of grievance demanding that all department orders be issued in writing "to minimize misunderstandings."

July 18   At the conclusion of the necessary three-day wait, Algernon takes the grievance to the second stage—the office manager—claiming that he has heard nothing from Gerry.

July 19   Gerry and Downey discuss the problem. Gerry thinks the grievance is a "lot of bunk." Algernon is just "trying to make trouble." Downey tries to "listen some reason into" Gerry's statement but feels he has failed.

July 21   Gerry still refuses to take any action. Algernon has asked that the grievance be taken to the third stage, Martin Gray.

July 22   Downey does take the grievance to Martin Gray. He has the choice of doing this himself or of letting the employee do it. He wants to stay on top of the problem, find a solution if possible. Gray asks that all four parties—Gray, Gerry, Algernon, and Downey—meet the following morning.

July 23   With Gray listening, all parties give their versions of the original incident. Gerry and Algernon defend their actions: "It was clearly communicated and then fouled up," says one. The other: "It was an honest misunderstanding growing out of a poor piece of communication. It should have been written down."

Gray agrees with Downey that both parties are in the wrong to some extent and hunts for a compromise solution: "Where important operating instructions are issued for the first time, or where they change a basic procedure, they will be put out in writing,"

Gray says. "Where they merely reinforce what has been done, or are not of such gravity as to require that they be put in writing, they will be given orally."

Gerry and Algernon accept the compromise and leave; Downey and Gray have a chance to talk over the problem of Gerry himself. They agree to a course of action involving, first, Gray's giving personal attention to Gerry—to the point where he will now talk with him regularly; second, Gerry, an outstanding technical man, will in a few weeks be encouraged to take a supervisor's course in interpersonal communications and human relations; and third, he will then be told that his chances of advancement depend on how well he applies the lessons, controls turnover (still much higher than in other departments) and other problems in his area, and cooperates with others around him.

So it was done. Under the polite pressure exerted by Gray, Gerry gradually came around. He even began to attend Downey's supervisors' meetings. Yet until some months later, when turnover and other problems had been brought under control in his department, and he received a healthy salary increase, he seemed to be concealing, poorly, some hostility toward Downey. After the raise, he became friendly. The bad apple had been made whole.

TEST-CASE SEQUEL

The test case cleared a lot of air. Both supervisors and non-exempt employees saw that management was willing and able to back up the complaint procedure. Employees realized that they had a forum in which to air complaints and solve grievances in an atmosphere of judicious examination.

Downey's stock rose steadily. He became the complete apostle of listening. More important, the tone changed in the Admin Building. Problems shrank in size and complexity. When Downey asked for, and obtained, a general increase for Admin Building employees the following January, half a dozen of them stopped by his office, at different times, to say thank you. One of them was Ann Furlong. "It's really changed around here in eight or nine months—thanks to you," she said. "Suddenly we know that someone around here likes us."

7

Because We Live Here

THE TWO EVENTS OCCURRED less than a week apart—almost as if they had been arranged that way by a capricious Providence. Hal Johnson, plant manager of the RJB Corporation's Jacktown facilities, suddenly saw his whole career going on the line in a matter of days.

First, the Main Office sent its two top troubleshooters, Al Ford and Pete Michaels, to "study the possibility that the Jacktown plant might have to relocate in a suburban area." Second, fulfilling an obligation that he had accepted well before the Ford/Michaels visit, Johnson gave a talk before the combined Jacktown Rotary and Kiwanis clubs.

At the closed-door relocation meeting, Johnson went strongly on record for retention of the Jacktown plant. "I know there's some deterioration taking place in the neighborhood," he said at one point. "But most of our people come from this area. They're good people and they don't want to see the neighborhood change any more than we do. They would work to solve the problems, I'm sure."

Al Ford put his finger on the heart of the problem facing corporate management. "The neighborhood is one thing," he said. "Our P&L statement is another. These buildings are old, which is no one's fault. The character of your workforce is changing as younger men and women come in, and as you say, most of them come from the area. But

152/Because We Live Here

the younger people don't work like the older ones. We're afraid you'll be seeing these and other factors create a real bind productionwise. You know, absenteeism, tardiness, poor quality—all the things that have killed us in other big-city areas like this."

Johnson stuck to his guns. "It won't kill us here," he insisted. "We can make this plant work with the people we can draw from the area."

In the end, the troubleshooters gave him a year. They would have set a shorter deadline for a final decision, they said, if Johnson had been on the job longer. But three months weren't enough; he had hardly gotten his feet wet in the plant manager's job and, frankly, his predecessor had let a lot of things slide.

So he had a year in which to prove that a plant could live in a changing, inner-city neighborhood.

The speaking engagement followed a few days later. Johnson had been discussing with a consulting firm the possibility that an employee interview program might help him keep current on worker sentiments and problems. Now, before the talk, he hired the firm and began a series of conversations with the firm's interviewer, Brent Alford, that proved a continuing, fruitful source of ideas. As a result of one of them, Johnson decided to make the speech the starting point of a campaign to renew public confidence in the future of Jacktown. The Jacktown plant could only benefit if such a campaign succeeded, Johnson reasoned.

From the 1,000-plus employees in the Jacktown plant, the main RJB facility producing heating/air conditioning equipment, Johnson selected three employees who agreed to attend a luncheon meeting with him. One was black, a second Caucasian, and the third Puerto Rican. Johnson wanted these employees, two men and a woman, to hear his call to the community. Beyond that he wanted to stress employee participation in everything, something his predecessor had never done.

THREE PRINCIPLES

The key portions of Johnson's talk made the local press. ". . .As the area's largest employer, we would like to state our creed and a challenge. Our creed, basically, rests on three key principles. First, our company, which draws its employees from this complex of communities, is inextricably a part of those communities. Second, management and worker are intimately tied up in the future of this area . . . in its viability, its success in meeting its problems. Third, we can and should exert all possible effort—more effort than ever before—to make the management-worker-community partnership a reality in new, creative ways.

"That's why I've introduced George Brown, Carmen Alvarez, and Alvin Parks to you today. I want you to see the people who make this area what it is, who can help us make it better. In our plant, people like these three are helping us with their ideas. Recently we started to seek those ideas actively by formally asking for them in employee meetings. Our plant is changing for the better and will change even more. I think the same type of thing can be done in the community. And that leads me to my challenge.

"I would like to suggest that we join forces to tap the creative forces in this area. If we can do that, I firmly believe a tremendous reservoir of creative input will be opened to us. Active participation will replace indifference. Civic and business organizations—your companies and businesses—will see their own efforts supplemented, abetted. *Everyone* will have a chance to take part in what could be the biggest thing to sweep through this community in all its history.

"I can't be totally certain about this, but I think some

of the social problems we've seen developing here will become solvable—the drug, delinquency, ecological, and other problems. Certainly every employer will see an increase in employee pride and spirit if we can change the community's mood and outlook.

"I'd like to see this start right now. I'd like to see it undertaken with the cooperation of all available constructive forces in the community.

"We, as a plant and company, live here. That's the best reason I can think of for promising my—*our*—full support. You want the place where you live to be the best possible."

Johnson sat down to a standing ovation. The campaign he had called for got under way that day; he was elected chairman of a committee charged with the responsibility of exploring possible avenues of approach.

Back in his office, he realized that he now faced a new challenge: How to mesh the community and company drives in such a way as to reap benefit for both. If one failed, the other probably would. The rebirth of civic or community pride that he sought might remain an unfulfilled dream; the in-plant improvement that he had to have would probably then elude him and the P&L would show it. Ford and Michaels would be back.

THE IDEA MILL

As plant manager, Johnson had introduced an "excitement factor" into the plant's situation. He used the same basic techniques that he had employed while working as a foreman years earlier. He trusted his people, he expected outstanding performance from them, and he let them know it; he listened carefully to ideas, no matter what their source; he moved fast when he saw possible advantage; and he was not afraid to take a chance. People working for him felt a kind of electricity when he was around; they felt as if they were working *with* him rather than *for* him.

The ideas began to pour in from the plant employees, requiring decisions. Each comment, each complaint, each suggestion brought in by Brent Alford received a full and honest answer; where action was possible, Johnson ordered it. In many cases, however, action was out of the question. Cost factors made some projects impossible; other suggestions conflicted with plans already in the works.

Choices began to open up to Johnson as he combed through the ideas that employees were submitting.

He could stress plant ecology if he so desired. Many of the ideas referred to housekeeping and maintenance problems, the appearance of the plant's two connecting buildings, similar subjects.

He could stress education and training as means to better communication and higher efficiency.

He encountered many suggestions centering on the need for new or more modern equipment and tools. Still others fell in the areas of supervision, employee benefits, special facilities, communications per se, and others.

He discussed the comments and suggestions with Alford.

"We have all kinds of ways to go," Johnson said. "We don't want to ignore any of them totally because then we show we're not listening. But I have the feeling we should choose one particular thing or area and stress it hard. Something symbolic, Something that'll make our people in the plant say, 'This company is serious. It means business. It's going to stay here and so am I, and we can make this business go and help the community improve too.' "

"They've definitely been wondering whether the plant would move or stay," Alford said. "We've picked up the rumors in interview sessions. But your speech has already done something to kill all that. The newspaper coverage was really beautiful."

"It's only a beginning, Brent. We've got to make this determination to stay and to operate successfully a real, live, continuing thing. Think about it, will you?"

"Sure. In the meantime, I think the foremen are beginning to open up more. They're tossing their ideas into the pot now. That means they're catching on to this listening business."

"Stay with them as much as with the hourly people. We're agreed that the foremen can make or break a program like this."

"TO PARTICIPATE IN OTHER WAYS. . ."

Alford became Johnson's eyes and ears as the search for a "beacon project" went on. Whatever that project might eventually be, it had to correlate with the feelings and sentiments of the workforce; it had to strike a responsive chord among both employees and citizens of the Jacktown area. It had to have true utility value; it would not be mere window-dressing. It had to have symbolic value as well, for otherwise it might remain noninspirational and pedestrian, another vacant-lot cleanup project that came and went without exciting anyone.

Excitement. That was the standard Johnson applied.

Neither Johnson nor Alford realized they were getting closer to an answer when one of the second-shift employees asked whether he could "come in early some day and put some of that waste paint on the walls of our department."

Alford asked; Johnson gave his permission. In a week the department had an entirely new look. Using random lots of paint of various colors, the employee, Hector Laguna, had covered all the walls of the department with brilliant, unusual designs. A thread of authentic artistic excellence unified what might otherwise have been a series of wild, esthetically invalid murals.

Johnson had pictures taken of the Laguna murals. Copies were posted on all the plant's bulletin boards. Employees from other departments came to gape, and Laguna's artistry had suddenly touched off an intraplant competition—again with Johnson's blessing.

The competition began with random requests, delivered at Alford's meetings, that other departments be allowed to decorate their walls. The requests came spontaneously. Groups of employees did the work in the other departments, working on their own time, either before or after their shifts.

Touring the plant as one of the competition judges after the murals were all done, Johnson sensed what had happened. His employees had fulfilled a desire to improve their workplaces. They had done it themselves. Using a few hundred dollars' worth of materials that might otherwise have had little or no genuine value, they had not merely beautified the plant; they had also expressed pride in it.

Extend that spirit to the community, or provide the opportunity to spread it into the community, and you probably had the answer to the need for a project. "They want to participate in other ways, not just to work here," Alford said later, expressing Johnson's feeling precisely. "That need exists in all workforces to a greater or lesser extent, but here it's a positive drive. They see participation as some kind of guarantee that they'll have jobs in the future, that the plant will stay here, if you want to put it bluntly."

"And once we make this kind of participation a long-term thing, a permanent thing, we will have given a final fillip to our quality, productivity, and other specifically production efforts?"

"Very likely."

THE GREAT ENLIGHTENMENT

The plant hummed with ideas in action. Four foremen were talking Spanish lessons so that they could converse more readily with their Spanish-speaking subordinates. A special quality program had been instituted, and already appeared to be getting results. Waste was declining. Training programs had been launched for new employees who did not have the qualifications for entry-level jobs. New communications efforts had been attempted as outgrowths of Alford's work with employees, including a daily bulletin that appeared each morning on plant bulletin boards.

Johnson's work with the Jacktown Improvement Committee was also beginning to show results. A preliminary survey had shown major areas of need: housing, the environment, jobs for young men and women, a concentrated attack on drug abuse. Programs were taking shape. Local businesses were being contacted en masse in an effort to enlist broad cooperation. But something, Johnson felt, was missing: the inspirational element, the excitement factor, the symbol.

One of the plant's black employees supplied the answer at one of Alford's meetings with employees.

"We've got a lot of people here who would like to work out in the community," Henry Pearson said that Tuesday morning. "What we need is a community center of some kind—you know, where people can gather, work, help out, maybe give classes, do all kinds of things."

Later in the day Alford and Pearson sat in Johnson's office, at Alford's request. Pearson repeated his suggestion. When he was finished, Johnson asked him questions: "Do others think this would be a good thing? There's something run by the city already, something along those lines—would we be in competition with that? Would many people take part, in your opinion?"

When Pearson had gone back to work, Johnson leaned back, smiling. "I think we've got it, Brent. This is the block-buster, the thing that will put us out in the community in a really useful way. Now I've got work to do."

The work proved exhausting. But at the end of 90 days Johnson had obtained approval from RJB corporate head-quarters to proceed with the idea. He also had a grant from headquarters of $25,000 for purchase of a building and installation of a few basic facilities.

The Jacktown Neighborhood Foundation was formed, with George Lyman, Johnson's second in command, as first president. Henry Pearson was named vice president.

Johnson broke the news of the project at a meeting of the Jacktown Improvement Committee.

"We've decided to go ahead with a special improvement project of our own," Johnson told the group of eight busi-nessmen of the community. "We've set up a foundation that will engage in a variety of projects. I have here a statement of basic goals that you may be interested in." Johnson passed out a sheaf of one-page summaries of the foundation's goals (Exhibit 7-1); as they circulated, each man taking one, he continued:

"Essentially, this project will involve setting up a neigh-borhood center open to anyone. We already have the building. Our own people will be helping out. They're very excited about it because it will give them a chance to get out in the community and do something concrete. And of course that's one of our goals, as you'll note on that sheet."

"We're hoping we can get more help from other firms in the area in making this foundation work. We see it as an inspirational thing, a project that can engage the services and assistance of almost anyone willing to help in any way. We also see it as a fountain of creative projects of one kind and another—classes, art or craft projects, counseling, and so on."

7-1. Statement of goals of Jacktown Neighborhood Foundation.

The following have been established as the basic goals of the Jacktown Neighborhood Foundation:
1. To institute a model of community action that will serve the dignity and worth of each individual taking part in the foundation's activities.
2. To provide a direct channel to Jacktown community residents of all ages so that as many as possible can be helped on a personal basis.
3. To help mobilize community action among the greatest possible number of RJB Jacktown plant employees and others who may want to assist in any way.
4. To establish a new, human approach to the solution of individual problems such as joblessness, lack of training; language, reading, and similar handicaps; day-care assistance, and so on.
5. To express the concern of RJB Jacktown plant management for the present improvement and future viability of the entire Jacktown community in line with the plant's role in the Jacktown Improvement Committee.
6. To forward, by direct action in the community, the fight against crime, juvenile delinquency, drug abuse, ecological decay, and other problems of the inner city.
7. To provide impetus for similar or complementary actions and efforts by other community firms and individuals.
8. To supplement services and facilities already provided by the city on a neighborhoodwide or local basis.

There were questions, comments:

"What possibilities do you see for participation by other companies in the area?"

"Absolutely unlimited," Johnson said. "We'd like to keep activities going all the time, if possible seven days a week."

"When do you plan to announce this to the press?"

"Right away. I wanted to go over it with the committee first to get all our ducks in a row. If possible, even though it's our show so far, I'd like to announce it as one phase of our activities as a member of the Improvement Committee. We want to tie in with the committee's work as closely as possible. I'd like to see if we can't spur a broader range of interpersonal activities."

"I really think you've found the way to do it," said Art Masters, owner of Masters Sporting Goods.

Listening, as the conversation became general, Johnson knew he had scored.

IMPLEMENTATION

The press again gave its full support to the neighborhood project. Johnson's name appeared repeatedly despite his attempts to spread the glory. In an interview he even gave credit to Henry Pearson for suggesting the Neighborhood Foundation in the first instance. The *Jacktown Times* reporter interviewed Pearson and wrote up the story of his contribution and of Alford's role in eliciting ideas from RJB Jacktown employees.

In the Improvement Committee, a movement started to take shape. Members thought the Jacktown plant's system might be extended to the community as a whole. A tentative project even received a tentative name: "What's the Big Idea?"

Johnson saw the plant and community efforts beginning to merge more and more. His own employees were volunteering in numbers to help carry out the foundation's work, and programs of various kinds had gone into planning. Most of these were the outgrowths of employee suggestions, and included such projects as classes for neighborhood girls who wanted to develop secretarial skills and the poise and confidence needed to put them to effective use, classes in both English and Spanish for persons not born to one or another of the languages, a cooperative program under which volunteers from the foundation's center worked in a local hospital, a day-care center for the children of working mothers, and an elderly-care program.

A group of Johnson's line employees volunteered to redecorate the center. Evenings, working as a team, they painted and scrubbed. The building had been a private home; an elderly widow had occupied it almost until the time of her death. She had been unable to keep it up, but underneath its superficial flaws it remained solid and livable. Visiting it near the end of the redecoration project, Johnson was impressed.

"It's going to look like a million dollars," he said to Lyman. "I think we should hold a grand opening and invite the neighborhood."

"You could also invite Ford and Michaels. They're due to make a visit here in a month." Lyman was smiling.

"You know," Johnson said, "I think I will. How else will they see what can be done in a concrete way in an area like this? We'll have some of the bigshots in the community, the people in the neighborhood—" He snapped his fingers. "You're a genius, George."

"And I think I've just talked myself into a job."

FOREMAN FEEDBACK

Johnson made it a practice to meet with his foremen at least twice a month. Many months, he held four, even five meetings. For the most part, the sessions were geared to discussion of a specific subject or problem, but sometimes Johnson called a meeting to obtain feedback. In such cases he simply allowed the conversation to drift where it would. He wanted to keep abreast of the thinking of his line foremen.

He decided to call what he termed a "nondirective" meeting after talking with Tommy Jarvis, one of the day foremen.

"You know, Hal," Jarvis had said, "some of the boys are saying we've sort of lost you—you're so busy with this community improvement stuff. Don't get me wrong. They believe it's the way to go, all right, but a few times recently when we've needed a top-level decision you've been out somewhere."

"It may be a justified gripe," Johnson had answered. "I'd better talk to them about it."

Johnson not only called the foremen meeting; he made it a platform for promulgation through action of his belief that the foremen held the key to establishment of an open, fully operative interpersonal communications atmosphere. As the foremen talked, he listened. The comments bore out what Jarvis had said.

"Hal," said Mick Jaworski, "I don't want to speak for the other guys here, but there's a feeling that when you spend more than, say, a morning away from the plant it makes problems for us here. Evenings—well, it wouldn't matter so much, even though Jim has to call you on one thing or another pretty often on the second shift. I guess you'd say the day-shift guys feel it the most."

"That's right, Hal." The speaker was Jerry Browning, one of the best foremen in the plant. "We had to make a quick decision the other day and tried to get you for some advice. Remember? We had to drop an order and switch over. You were at a meeting at the time."

"You made the right decision, Jerry, if that's any consolation," Hal said. "Any other comments?"

Others spoke, citing instances. When they had concluded, Hal spoke again. "I've got a fine line to walk here, as you gents know," he said. "I need your advice. That's why we're here, in fact. Believe me, this problem is one that has caused me concern. But the question is—or, rather, the two questions I have to ask are: Is it worth it to help push this whole community project? And, second, how much time away is enough and how much is too much? I don't have the answers yet myself. But I plan to find them. Meantime, you can answer this: Have we accomplished anything?"

"If you mean with the people, the answer is a big yes," Jerry said. "They're as excited as a bunch of kids with a new playground."

"Have we seen any improvement in quality, productivity—that kind of thing—where it can show?"

"You're damn tootin'," Jarvis said. "That's not the point. They're bustin' their backs for this place now. They've always been good workers, on average, but now—well, they feel it's more like a family, I guess. No, this is our problem, and I think everyone will agree on that."

"I'll promise this, then. I'll spend less time outside, but I'll have to spend *some* to keep things moving. And we'll meet in a month to go over this again."

They were talking animatedly when they left.

DAY OF TRUMPETS

The day of the grand opening and the open house social was what Johnson liked to think of as a day of trumpets: a day of triumph and rejoicing on which community-plant solidarity achieved full expression.

The formal ceremonies were mercifully brief, but they provided the colorful kickoff for the open house that followed. · Attending were the Jacktown plant's employees, many of whom had contributed, or were contributing, energy and ideas to the center; members of the Improvement Committee; many merchants and shopkeepers of the area, and Ford and Michaels, representatives of the RJB Corporation's main office. Under the slogan "Because We Live Here," the program included four talks, music by the Jacktown High School Marching Band, a ceremonial ribbon cutting, and the open house itself.

Ford and Michaels were impressed. Going over the plant's situation and record in Johnson's office later, they admitted as much. They had been accorded an exhibition of showmanship, but they had seen, underneath the trappings, the signs of plant and community spirit that they were looking for.

"You've got only a few months to go on your year," Michaels told Johnson, "but you're going to make it. I can feel it."

"Don't think we're doing all this without keeping an eye on those numbers there," Johnson said, indicating the production and other reports that Michaels had been studying, "We've become convinced that one good way to a workforce's heart is through its backyard, that's all."

Ford spoke. "Your experience here may hold a lesson for some other corporation plants, Hal. How would you like to sketch out some guidelines that others might be able to use?"

"Will do, tonight. I'll ship them along to you. They'll be brief and to the point."

"That's what we want."

That evening Hal listed ten guideposts to a successful community relations drive (Exhibit 7-2). He sent them along

7-2. Ten guideposts to a successful community relations drive.

1. Start with a bang. In civic movements the race is not to the timid.
2. Obtain the broadest possible participation at the earliest possible date, stressing participation by employees as well as others in the community.
3. Get an organization behind the movement from the start, or as early as possible. Become active in the organization if possible.
4. Set realistic goals and tailor programs to move toward those goals.
5. Take an objective look from time to time at what has been accomplished.
6. Divide the work so that no single individual bears too much of the burden—at the top of the effort or the bottom.
7. Employ publicity in every legitimate way to spread information on the community relations program or on specific activities and projects.
8. Credit employees and others with accomplishments where such credit is due.
9. Be flexible in working toward your goals; keep them general until you see what people will be capable of achieving.
10. Listen to ideas on all sides, weigh them and honor each with an answer, put into effect those that are feasible and that promise constructive results.

to Ford. Two weeks later, the main office issued a memo to all operating staffs in plants around the country (Exhibit 7-3). The memo called on plant managements to take aggressive action, within the limits set by practical considerations such as funds and time, to cement relations with local communities. Urban plants were urged particularly to take a forward look and to do all in their power to ally themselves with constructive forces in their communities.

The experience of the Jacktown plant was cited specifically as a model of action promising a generous measure of success. Johnson's ten guideposts were appended to the memo because of "their possible value in helping conceptualize and formulate programs of community relations."

Johnson showed the memo to Lyman. "This should go out to all our employees, at least in some form," Johnson said. "How about this for the plant paper: Jacktown Plant Singled Out for Excellence of Community Relations Program"?

"Great," Lyman said. He was smiling as he read the memo. "But the headquarters memo doesn't mention our employees."

"No, but we have to. They're the ones we're really trying to reach, not headquarters."

7-3. Introduction to RJB Corporation memo on community relations programs.

With popular attention focused on pollution, racial integration, and similar issues, industry as a whole and individual plants in particular have come under severe attack. To date none of our divisions or plants has been made the target of a public campaign, but positive action is called for

7-3 (Cont.)

where such is deemed necessary to forestall negative or destructive approaches. Our paper mill operation in Seaville, to name only one operation, has succeeded in retaining a favorable public image by taking aggressive action to police and purify its effluent into the Muddy River.

On a more positive side, it is felt that major advantage can accrue to divisions or individual plants if managements can extend their community relations programs as widely as possible. Our desire is to formally encourage managements to launch or expand such programs with the aim of building plant/community solidarity, improving conditions in home communities, and instilling in employees pride and dedication to both community and their work.

The experience of our Jacktown facility, where Hal Johnson is plant manager, offers an example of community relations activity that will be instructive particularly to plants located in older urban areas. A good working relationship between plant and community, dovetailed with a very active community relations program and an internal communications program, has had positive effects in Jacktown on production, productivity, and other indices of operating effectiveness.

8

Motivation in the Research Lab

THE SOUND OF A GLASS RETORT shattering on the lab floor cleared Jim Elliott's brain. That, at least, was how he came to view the situation later.

The day had started poorly, no matter how you looked at it, and continued downhill. Elliott, head of the RJB Corporation's Research Lab, Chemical Division, had spent the morning getting advice from a variety of people in the division's hard-nosed line management group. The advice ran the gamut from "Get tough, Jim" to "Why don't you get rid of half of those chemist goldbricks?" Jim was still pondering what action he could take, if any, when in the afternoon of that sticky summer day the retort hit the floor.

Jim didn't actually hear the noise of the breaking glass, but he could hear the sound in his imagination as he tried to reconstruct the day's events in the lab. As far as he could tell they went as follows:

☐ Art Mueller, Elliott's assistant and a graduate of the line management ranks, asks Joe Rei, chemist-researcher, how Joe is coming on the 291-additive job. Joe apparently bristled and said, in effect, "You'd better decide whether you want that job done first or the one for Tom Benedetti. I've got to work on one or the other if I'm going to finish either."

☐ At 2:36 P.M. Mueller and Rei clash again. Mueller has come around to look for a piece of equipment, Rei is just going on his break; he is six minutes late already and gives Mueller a short answer.

□ Mueller, unable to find the piece of equipment after a ten-minute search, goes to the vending cafeteria and asks Rei if he's "just about finished in here." Rei had been reading a set of specs; these he now rolls up angrily. He follows Mueller back to the process lab. Three other researchers are there, all busily at work in various parts of the big room. As Mueller enters, followed by Rei, a glass retort crashes to the floor. No one is near the spot where it has fallen. As Mueller comes up to what is left of the retort, he sees that this is the piece of equipment he was looking for earlier.

The case reached Elliott three minutes later: Mueller entered Elliott's office in a rage. Elliott, roly-poly, shrewd of eye and mind, watched and listened as Mueller charged that someone had thrown the retort in outright defiance of his, Mueller's, authority. "They're full of tricks like this," Mueller said. "I wish they'd use half that creativity on their work."

"They don't?" Elliott asked. "We get complaints about delivery times, but never about their talents."

"Well, you're getting one from me now. I think you should weed half of them out."

"Sure, and fall ten times as far behind." Elliott thought a moment. "Let's go down to the lab and talk to those guys," he said finally. "This has aroused my curiosity."

"You go," Mueller said. "They won't talk if I'm there."

DEMOTIVATED EQUALS DEFIANT

Elliott went alone. He talked to the lab people—and listened to them. Gradually, he saw an ugly picture emerging, one whose dimensions surprised and worried him. In essence, he faced a motivational crisis in the process lab and, by implication, in all the rest of the Research Lab's various sections. Continuing his discussions on succeeding days, he confirmed the original finding.

Seventy-six researchers, all chemists except for a few technicians who served as their aides—this was the population of Elliott's domain. And from one border to another, all through this beautiful new building housing the Research Lab, the 76 citizens were in simmering rebellion. From Mueller himself came evidence of what Elliott's second in command considered sabotage:

March 18: A costly oven goes out of action. In making repairs a maintenance man finds some wires torn out.

April 10: An experimental mixture of caustics that promised to have potential as elements of industrial cleaners is mysteriously spilled. The researcher's notes have disappeared.

June 22: Eyeglass cleaners in a dispenser are strewn all over the floor one morning.

Elliott had left administrative details within the Research Lab to Mueller but now he decided to become more directly involved. The complaints he was hearing in face-to-face meetings reached all across the facility's spectrum of activities and policies (see Exhibit 8-1). They clearly called for corrective action, but first, Mueller felt, he had to understand completely what was happening.

The chemists themselves filled in most of the details. They seemed to have gone sour two years before, when this new facility had first opened. What should have given them new pride in their work along with added motivation had had no such effect; on the contrary, the quality of their work seemed to have suffered. Researchers mentioned no names and cited few specific instances, but indicated in their specification of key problem areas that they were hampered particularly by red tape, inadequate supervision, the continual

8-1. Major problem areas mentioned by Research Lab chemists.

1. Inadequate salaries.
2. Poor advancement potential. Opportunities should be opened up to enable lab personnel to move into more demanding and higher-paying jobs or levels of management.
3. The need for regular, sure channels of downward and upward communication. In particular, opportunity to talk to the facility manager, such as has been provided recently, should be expanded.
4. The need to recognize individuality and to give oral or written recognition where it is deserved.
5. The need for reinforcement of the "professionalism" of lab personnel at all levels, establishment and upgrading of their status, encouragement of further development, and provision of more time for creative research.
6. The need for top-flight, knowledgeable supervision; review of the whole management structure in the facility.
7. The need for ways to settle grievances and complaints quickly and equitably.
8. The need to foster continued and expanded identification of lab personnel with management in all possible ways.
9. The need for wider personal responsibility in the conduct of specific projects and the reduction of red tape.
10. The need to insure uniform and prompt discharge of administrative and personnel functions, including merit appraisals.
11. Less than adequate working conditions.
12. The need for more formal communication on policy and other matters dealing directly with the Research Lab.

need to race the clock to get out routine jobs, and lack of communication.

Elliott added some other details. The table of organization at whose pinnacle he sat showed four levels of managerial and supervisory responsibility: his own; Mueller's, as deputy manager; three floor supervisors, one to each floor; and eleven group leaders, one to each group of four to nine chemists. The men holding the latter two types of job appeared to speak the same language. They talked of quotas and deadlines; they spoke of unending pressure to get jobs out on time, as did Mueller himself.

Until the Mueller-retort incident, Elliott, too, had thought in terms of production targets, deadlines, delivery dates. But he saw that his chemists did not, could not, think entirely in those terms. The crash of the retort—and Elliott had to admit private admiration for the ingenuity of the man who had rigged the retort so he could have it crash when Mueller reentered the room—had served as a signal of defiance, of desperation. Talking to these creative men, Elliott saw them in a new light. He decided that he had to take back the reins from Mueller; he had to make changes; he had to stay in close contact with the psychological atmosphere of the facility.

DOUBLE DUTY

The research facility, Elliott had been told when he was named to manage it, had a twofold mission: to conduct applied research and to engage in creative or pure research. The former responsibility involved developmental work on existing plastics and other materials, usually in response to very specific descriptions of need from customers, salesmen, and others. The second function was stated in vague terms: between applied research projects, the chemists were to be allowed to engage in creative work of possible major value to the Chemical Division and the company as a whole. The first task had obviously swallowed up the latter, as comments from the chemists made clear:

□ "You don't get to do any real research around here—no creative work. You're always chasing some job that should have been turned in yesterday."

□ "We were hired to do some pure research, some applied research. It just doesn't happen that way."

□ "If you try to do your own research projects, even on your own time, they holler at you to go and get the latest emergency out."

Worse, perhaps, a system of controls had been instituted to perpetuate the imbalance between the two kinds of research. The entire management structure seemed geared to the role of policing and pressuring; that was the impression that came through to Elliott as the chemists talked. He knew there must be some exaggeration here. But was there, really? The chemists' perceptions of the situation represented reality to *them*. The evidence that the facility had reached an impasse, with both subordinates and supervisors embattled in defense of their own positions, came out of contrapuntal comments from the group leaders and the chemists:

Group leaders: "We have to bear down on this reporting all the time. Otherwise it just goes by the board." "They fight it even though it gives us something to go on when we're making out performance appraisals." "They're against the reporting even though we have to have it when *we're* asked where various projects are."

Chemists: "These documents and papers we have to make out—they're strictly Mickey Mouse." "We spend hours every week just making out reports and papers when we could be doing research jobs, important ones." "This reporting just makes everyone mad. We're buried in paperwork."

THE CONTROL SYNDROME

Elliott probed the number and nature of the controls exercised in the facility. He probed both among those enforcing the controls and those subject to them. The controls did not seem that numerous, but they were certainly all-pervasive: A report, for example, had to be made out each time a job moved into a new stage even though the new stage might involve a minor change of procedures. There were weekly reports, monthly reports, group reports, and others.

Other controls applied to the chemists' personal schedules. They had to be at work at a given time and had to work through until a specified quitting time. They had definite break times, which were honored in the breach as much as in the observance. They had to report to a group leader if they wanted to go out of their assigned work areas. They could be docked if they overstayed their lunch periods.

Knowing the job of the lab and the types of controls in effect, Elliott set to work to find guidance. He found plenty of indications that the typical research facility had fewer controls than his own operation. The organizational structure of a "typical" facility was loose and flexible. But did that typical—and perhaps mythical—facility have a heavy load of production-oriented tasks? That was the key question. Even while pondering it, Elliott could see what the control syndrome had wrought in the RJB Research Lab:

□ The double research task of the Research Lab had become a single one: to carry out the applied research or production-oriented jobs exclusively.

□ A relatively complex organization had grown up, or been planted, in the Research Lab, with directive management standards and techniques more common to a manufacturing facility applied up and down the management line.

□ The ideas turned in by Research Lab chemists were

rarely if ever acted on, with the result that such ideas had become almost extinct.

□ In line with the behavioral scientists' predictions, the resentments of the researchers had become focused on the enforcers of controls—the group leaders, the floor supervisors, and Mueller himself.

□ The creative process had gone entirely by the boards in the Research Lab, and the chemists had, as they insisted, become flunkies of the manufacturing side.

Talking it over with Mueller, Elliott met raw opposition to the very idea of change.

"We'll blow the whole thing sky-high," Mueller said, "if we give these guys an inch. This system's been here and functioned for a long time. It's working. The men know what to expect. Its operations are ingrained in our group leaders."

"Do we have to be carried along by it even though we see signs that it's having bad effects?"

"That retort? That's minor. You've got to look at the whole picture. How do you plan to meet our schedules if you give these guys any kind of freedom?"

The phrase "these guys," a reference to the chemists, had begun to irritate Elliott. He had to evolve a plan, and he had to get acceptance of it from Larry Stack, works manager.

THE TASK-ORGANIZATION-PEOPLE FIT

Elliott came across an article in *Harvard Business Review*. There it was: the Idea.

In arguing for an approach which emphasizes the fit among task, organization, and people, we are putting to rest the question of which organizational approach—the classical or the participative— is best. In its place we are raising a new question: what organizational approach is most appropriate given the task and the people involved?

For many enterprises, given the new needs of younger employees for more autonomy, and the rapid rates of social and technological change, it may well be that the more participative approach is the most appropriate. But there will still be many situations in which the more controlled and formalized organization is desirable. Such an organization need not be coercive or punitive. If it makes sense to the individuals involved, given their needs and their jobs, they will find it rewarding and motivating.*

Elliott read the study through again from the beginning. He noted the table in the article, in which the differences in "climate" characteristics in two high-performing organizations were enumerated (shown in Exhibit 8-2). He took particular note of the finding that *both* organizations, one with a relatively authoritarian structural orientation and the other with a more flexible, participative structure, were successful in the performance of their basic missions.

Why not seek a middle ground for the Research Lab? Its potential mix of production-oriented work and pure research might thus be converted to reality. The mix might initially have to be weighted heavily in favor of production-oriented work, if only to avert the day of doom that Mueller foresaw; but if it worked, the jobs would go out faster, the work would be done better, and defiant attitudes would dwindle. The researchers would become actual participants in the work of the lab instead of drudges who came and went without a forward or backward look, *without caring.*

Elliott went to see Stack. But first he consolidated his thoughts on future directions for the Research Lab: What controls would go, what new policies or guidelines might be instituted, what training programs might be inaugurated to

*John J. Morse and Jay W. Lorsch, "Beyond Theory Y," *Harvard Business Review,* May-June 1970, p. 68.

8-2. Differences in climate in high-performing organizations.

CHARACTERISTIC	AKRON	STOCKTON
1. Structural orientation.	Perceptions of tightly controlled behavior and a higher degree of structure.	Perceptions of a low degree of structure.
2. Distribution of influence.	Perceptions of low influence, concentrated at upper levels in the organization.	Perceptions of high total influence more evenly spread out among all levels.
3. Nature of superior-subordinate relations.	Low freedom vis-à-vis superiors to choose and handle jobs, directive type of supervision.	High freedom vis-à-vis superiors to choose and handle projects, participatory type of supervision.
4. Nature of colleague relations.	Perceptions of many similarities among colleagues, high degree of coordination of colleague effort.	Perceptions of many differences among colleagues, relatively low degree of coordination of colleague effort.
5. Time orientation.	Short term.	Long term.
6. Goal orientation.	Manufacturing.	Scientific.
7. Top executive's managerial style.	More concerned with task than people.	More concerned with task than people.

Source: John J. Morse and Jay W. Lorsch, "Beyond Theory Y," *Harvard Business Review*, May–June 1970, p. 66.

indoctrinate the Research Lab's management staff, and so on. As he walked the long block to the Chemical Division's front gate, and heard the rumble of the huge kettles, a physical sensation in the feet, he felt qualms. Was he lost in a world of theory? Was Mueller the one who was in touch with reality?

After a pause, he continued on. Life was full of risk.

THE GUIDELINES

Stack seized on the two key questions almost at once: How do you get your management people to go along? How do you control change once it has been set in motion—and keep the work flowing?

To the first, Elliott had an answer ready: you lay down guidelines, you educate the group leaders in what is expected of them, and then you watch and listen carefully to make sure your ideas are being put into effect. The process was comparable to what was done in the plant itself; management *could* color, if not prescribe in every detail, what the foremen did, could it not?

Stack laughed. "I don't know," he said, "whether we lead them, and guide them, and create the plant's atmosphere, or whether *they* lead us and create the climate they want. But go ahead; what guidelines do you have in mind?"

Elliott produced them (see Exhibit 8-3). He watched while Stack read. At the end, Stack laid the papers on his desk and swiveled his chair so that he was facing the window. It provided a view across a truck yard to the sheet-metal buildings that house the kettles. Stack was thoughtful. "It's pretty daring," he said finally. "You realize, of course, that you might have to make some personnel changes if you attempt that kind of change of direction?"

"I've thought of the possibility." Elliott was thinking of Mueller. "But I'd like to cross that bridge when I come to it.

8-3. Guidelines for management personnel, RJB Research Lab.

The following guidelines for management personnel in the RJB Corporation Research Lab will become effective immediately. Management personnel, including group leaders, will refer to the guidelines in all matters touching on relations with chemist-researchers. Discussion sessions, training seminars, and other means will be employed to make the operational significance of the guidelines clear.

1. Every effort will be made to understand the need for creativity and for giving full play to the creative process in the day-to-day discharge of functions.
2. Communication with creative personnel, including researcher-chemists, will be considered a special challenge that every individual in management will be expected to master.
3. A fundamental task in the communication context will be to give recognition and credit where such is merited.
4. Listening of a professional nature will set the tone for each manager's communication style.
5. A basic assignment for every individual in management will be to encourage and inspire subordinates to greater efforts.
6. Means of achieving organizational flexibility will be sought; as often as possible, they will be introduced in followup to the suggestions and ideas of both management and research personnel.
7. To the greatest extent possible, researchers will be given the freedom to pursue their own theories and methods in the discharge of their daily duties.
8. Management personnel will be required to study and understand, insofar as possible, the techniques and processes employed by researchers.
9. On the principle that there is some risk in pursuing any line of research, management personnel will be asked to encourage calculated risks, particularly where pure research projects are concerned.
10. Management personnel will be asked to keep abreast of problems in their areas and to keep the facility manager informed of such problems where they develop.

Meantime, every kind of reeducation would be attempted."

"OK, what about this business of getting the work out, keeping up with our needs here?"

"I think after a shakedown period we'll be able to do that better. You know my feeling; I think we've got tons of unused potential in that building."

"Could be. But you must also be aware that in the plant here the general approach is what someone called KITA— pretty authoritarian management?"

"I know it."

"You think the two systems, your proposed one and the one our guys use, could exist side by side?"

"I think so. If we were on the premises here, I'd be hesitant. But we're down the street."

THE GREAT EXPERIMENT

Stack had started in the Chemical Division at age 19, 42 years earlier. He had risen from the ranks of hourly employees to become works manager on the basis of his ability to manage men and get work out. Now he revealed a side to his philosophy whose existence Elliott had not suspected.

"Try it," he said, "what the hell do we have to lose? I've often wondered if our management techniques here in the division were the right ones. But you know how it is—you can't fight the tide. You go along. It'll be refreshing to see something new tried. Just keep me informed, would you? You know what kind of flak I'll get."

"Sure will." Elliott gathered his papers and left.

Monday of the following week he started his experiment. He chose the Monday morning staff meeting as the moment for facing the truth.

The meeting began in confusion and ended in heated discussion, with argument and counterargument flying in rapid succession. Mueller elected to take the oppositional lead.

"Hell, Jim," he said, "if we try this namby-pamby stuff, they not only won't know what we're trying to do, they'll wonder if we're trying to put one over on them."

"Not after you and I get done talking to them they won't. They've got to hear it spelled out in every miserable detail."

"You and I—?" Mueller was wide-eyed. "You mean *you*."

"I mean *you and I*. We'll talk for the next three days if necessary, but we've both got to understand it, and push it. So does every man here. So does every chemist and so does every technician before we finish."

Dixie Lawton, one of the group leaders, spoke up. "What does this part about looking for ways to achieve organizational flexibility mean?"

"It means," Elliott answered, "that over time we may make some organizational changes, loosen things up. But remember: We aren't going in with an ax. We're just trying to find a way to get these guys working because they want to work."

DENOUEMENT

The meeting lasted an hour and a half. When it was over, Elliott had gone over every point on his list of guidelines. He had discussed his new theory of management and argued down objections that "we won't be able to get a damn thing out on time," "these guys will be tearing this building apart," and "it's going to be open season on group leaders." He had made some inroads into the hard, harsh geography of his management team's attitudes. He had used that word more than once.

"It's *attitude* that's going to make or break this place," he said once. "*Your* attitude, *my* attitude. I'll be frank. I want to make you see this thing my way and to give this new program a fair chance. Without that, well—we're wasting a lot of time on nothing."

Listening to his own words, he heard what amounted to an implied threat, one that suggested that any man who did not go along with his program would not last very long. He left it that way. He had no promises to make and could not predict how he would feel in 30 or 60 days.

Inevitably, when he talked with the chemists in groups during the course of the week, the word was out. The grapevine had carried it through the building within half an hour after the Monday morning meeting. Elliott didn't care about that; he had known in advance that it would happen that way. By his reading of the situation, he still had to speak to every man in the lab in a face-to-face session; he had to lay out the promise and the possible penalty for failure; he had to personally seek the cooperation of every man. He used one statement with all the groups:

"We've been given a chance to set this place up on a new basis, to make it like a real research organization rather than a jail. It's going to take work on everybody's part."

Days passed. Weeks. Two of the group leaders asked for transfers back into the line jobs they had held earlier in the Chemical Division. Elliott hastened to comply with the requests and did not fill the two vacancies. Asked about it by the chemists, he said: "We're trying to let a little air in here, to get a looser organizational pattern. But you have my promise that when I do fill a management vacancy, one of you guys will get the nod. It wouldn't hurt if one or two of you with that kind of ambition started studying."

Eventually, Mueller also asked for a transfer back to the division. He had learned to keep his mouth shut, but he had never gone along with the new dispensation. Day in and day out, Elliott felt him gritting his teeth and chafing at the changes that began to flood into the lab: a guaranteed one-day-a-week allowance of time to every chemist for theoretical research, a new set of greatly simplified paper control and reporting forms that the chemists had suggested, a system of awards for achievement "above and beyond the call," and a slate of training sessions for management personnel and chemists alike.

Elliott reported regularly to Stack. But when Joe Rei came up with the idea for a new plastic powder mixture that promised to make obsolete at least four existing product lines, Elliott took Rei with him to see Stack in person.

"I think Joe's got something here," Elliott told Stack, "and he developed it himself. Here's our whole test book on it. Do you think manufacturing could dry-run it?"

Stack studied the papers. Finishing, he whistled softly. "Not only that," he said, "I think Sales had better get in on this from the word go." He looked at Elliott and Rei. "You know, I haven't had a single bitch from the line about your delivery schedules for two months. And now this. You've made it work."

"I didn't," Elliott said. "Joe and his buddies did."

Rei was smiling. He was a man who seldom smiled.

9

Communication in Black and White

FREEMAN JONES HAD PLAYED FOOTBALL.   Also, he was a good worker.   Some said later that the two didn't go together, and took that as prima facie evidence that Jones should have been fired after he mouthed off to Merck Balasanter, his foreman on the night shift.

Merck, filling in for Tommy Luciano, had been looking for someone to work the loading dock, where a shipment of metal sat awaiting attention.   It was five in the morning, and few members of the truncated third shift were around. Merck didn't know where they were.   They could have been anywhere in this antique, ramshackle, wandering facility that looked as if it had been hurled together by a revenge-seeking dropout from the Bauhaus.

Anyway, Freeman Jones was at his drill press when Merck approached him. Boxes of work sat next to Freeman—enough and plenty more to spare to keep him going full blast until the seven-thirty day shift came on.

"Jones," Merck said in his characteristically blunt way, "I want you to go out in back and help unload a truckload of metal."   He had a clipboard in his hand and had begun to scribble on it as if Jones's departure for the loading dock were already an accomplished fact.

"I can't go out there," Jones said.   "You know Blanton told me to stay at this stack of boxes until quittin' time."

"Blanton's second-shift supervisor, not foreman on the third shift, and he ain't here, and I *am* foreman on this shift; I've got to get that goddam truck unloaded and you're going to help do it."

"No, I'm not."

The RJB Corporation's lone metal-stamping unit—this ancient facility that consisted of no less than eight formerly independent, adjoining buildings—had been the scene of incidents like this before. But this scene was probably freer of interfering noise or distraction than the others. The two men simply faced each other, Jones with his hands still locked at the wrists into the safety cuffs, Merck Balasanter standing there with his clipboard. There were no witnesses.

Jones said later that Merck had called him a goddam nigger. Merck denied it. But the man stayed at his job, and the foreman, *at the end of the shift,* wrote him up and recommended suspension, meaning, in this plant, termination.

WORD AGAINST WORD

"We should drop the lousy shift," said Minie Crane, general manager. He was twisting his head and shaking it as if to rid himself of the constant stream of problems that the third shift represented.

"No, please. Let me check it out and get back to you," said Gene Kellogg, personnel director.

They were talking in Crane's office. The incident had occurred four hours earlier, and both principals were home. But Merck had stayed around after shift's end to present his case and his written account to Crane personally.

"It's one man's word against another, even if Jones denies it, and he will." Crane was angry, eager to get to something constructive. But Kellogg would not let go.

"There's more to this than meets the eye," Kellogg observed. "Jones has been our best, sometimes our only, worker on that shift. He's been considered for foreman, as you know. I'm just not going to take this bitch report at face value."

"But I've got to suspend the man. He was insubordinate."

"Suspend him one day. A token. Then I will have been able to talk to both parties."

"OK, but give me a clean report *and* a recommendation. By—" Crane looked at his watch, checking the date, "by Friday morning at this time. I want no favoritism, no racism, no ism of any kind. Forget the man's black. If he should be canned, I want you to say so."

"If he should be, I'll say so."

Kellogg left. In the ensuing 24 hours, working nearly around the clock, he had tied together a lot of details about the third shift. It began at 12:30 A.M. But it had a reputation among the second-shift workers as a goldbricker's paradise. There were reports, difficult to verify but equally difficult to disprove, that men and women on the third shift clocked in and simply disappeared. Some went home; some went to a nearby bar and drank the night hours away; some went to a small, locked room at the far east end of the building, gained entrance by whatever means, and slept. As evidence of the latter, Kellogg found rags on the floor of the storage room; the rags had been fashioned into a crude bed.

Kellogg was seeking facts, not gossip, and he unearthed much that was factual about the six-hour shift. For one thing, its productivity record was unbelievably low. For another, the seven white workers on the shift were in constant conflict with the 11 black employees. At least two or three times the subsurface conflict had erupted into fighting and name-calling. Each time, a foreman had broken it up simply by making an appearance, whereupon all the parties concerned denied that anything was occurring beyond a friendly conversation.

The reports of conflict troubled Kellogg the most. They echoed reports of incidents on the first and second shifts, incidents that often seemed to have a racial cast. But supervision on the day and afternoon shifts had been selected more carefully; and while the level of supervisory competence in the plant remained low, the night-shift supervisors were far and away the poorest in the plant. Rumors—and in some cases specific reports—suggested that these supervisors sometimes smelled strongly of liquor during their lonely, undoubtedly frustrating working hours.

Kellogg used the investigation as the rationale for exploring a whole range of questions bearing on the black—white problem. He talked with workers, both black and white. He caught foremen in unguarded moments and obtained answers that he otherwise never would have heard, and eventually he put together a picture of a deeply troubled workforce that needed—what? He didn't know yet, but some of the comments from workers gave him clues:

A black worker: "The company never tells us anything. The white guys seem to have all the news and we're left on the outside."

A white worker: "They should look at this whole policy of hiring blacks on an equal basis with whites. It's going to blow up one of these days; you won't be able to do anything about it. That'll be the day when the blacks outnumber us."

A black worker: "Look at who your foremen are—your group leaders. They're all white. What kind of a setup is that for us? Where can you get to in this place?"

A white woman married to a black man employed in another plant: "I can't blame the black people for being dissatisfied here. There's a lot of talk about equality, but it's not very real."

A supervisor: "We almost had a battle royal at the time clock the other day. Those Italian girls who've been getting to the clock first for years were beaten out by three or four black girls. It was all I could do to stop it. I just kept them from signing out until they quieted down and joined the line—quietly."

A black worker: "Why won't they let us put names on the stamping machines? We work them all the time. How could that hurt anybody?"

Up to this point Kellogg, the incumbent in the personnel director's job in this metal-stamping plant for four and a half months, had been swamped with the details of bringing order out of the records chaos left by his departed, unmourned predecessor. The plant itself had been part of the RJB Corporation complex for slightly over four years, and its policy on integration of black workers into the workforce was exactly that old. Kellogg was finding that the policy was a paper one; it existed in writing, not in reality.

RECOMMENDATION AND RESPONSE

Friday morning, before finishing his report for Minie Crane, Kellogg came in early, at 6:30 A.M. Luciano was still sick, and Balasanter was still filling in for him. When Kellogg went out into the plant, the foreman's balding head could be seen bent over his desk in the floor office. The glass walls of that office had been the idea of a general manager who had preceded Minie by some years.

Fifty feet from the office sat Freeman Jones, hard at work at No. 3 punch press. He had had his day off and had returned to work—so Kellogg had been told by Balasanter—"more sullen than ever." Kellogg approached the powerfully built black worker from the rear, waited until he finished a box of stampings that would soon be gun parts, and then spoke his name.

Jones turned, surprised, then smiled. "It's you, Mr. Kellogg. I thought it would be—." He did not finish his sentence.

"No, no one else. I was just wondering if you'd have a few minutes to stop in my office when the shift is over."

"Sure. Be glad to. It'll be another hour."

"Fine."

The two men had spoken at length earlier in the week. A bond of something akin to trust had developed in that one meeting, primarily, Kellogg thought, because he had let Jones tell his whole story without interruption.

When Jones came into his office shortly after 7:30, Kellogg was finishing his report for Minie Crane. He set the report aside, said, "Have a chair, Freeman," and went on: "I have a couple of questions that I'd like to put to you."

Kellogg asked his questions. First, did Jones plan to stay with the company? Receiving a positive answer, Kellogg moved on to his second question: If given the chance, would Jones move to the second shift, or to the first? Again a positive answer, very strong this time.

"I don't see much of a future on that third shift," Jones said, smiling.

Kellogg thanked Jones and the latter left. Kellogg went down to Minie's office with the finished report.

Minie was on a long-distance call, but called Kellogg in and had him wait while the call was completed. Hanging up, Crane said simply, "Well?"

Kellogg dropped the report on Crane's desk. "I'm absolving Jones of exclusive blame in that incident the other night," he said. "I'm also suggesting that you drop the third shift entirely if that can be squared with your operational needs. If you do that, you should give maybe half a dozen people now on the third shift the option of taking layoff or going on the second or first shifts. These are good people and we don't want to lose them."

Minie was reading the report. "You're also suggesting that we go into a full-scale human relations program, including training for all foremen, and a communications program. You going to run all this?"

"I certainly am. This is the most important thing we can do right now. That plant is seething out there."

"I've heard of incidents—but seething?"

"Seething. I hate to say it, because I think unions are great in their place, but you're going to have one pretty soon if we don't get on this right away. I'll stake my life on it."

"All we need is a union for our foremen to go completely out of their minds."

"Right. But you and I both know our foremen are making a lot of their own problems."

"I know." Minie's voice was dry. In a different tone he said: "Let me think this over for a day, will you?"

"How about the whole weekend?"

Kellogg was in his office Monday when Crane called. "I've done some checking on my own," Crane said, "over the weekend. I think your assessment of the situation is accurate, and I'm a little hot that I didn't get it from my foremen directly. But that's neither here nor there. I think you should go ahead full steam, but let's take it a bite at a time. What should we do first?"

"The foreman training program. Let's get it off the ground."

"Go. Just give me a sketch, or plan, or something so I'll know what we're doing and won't sound dumb when someone asks about it."

"Will do."

"By the way, I'm knocking out the third shift as of a

week from Friday. I think we'll more than make up what we lose by offering late overtime to the second shift and pre-shift overtime to the day crew."

"My idea exactly. But you won't even find some of them in time to tell them they're laid off."

BRINGING A POLICY TO LIFE

Kellogg started to work immediately. His first task, he saw, was to obtain Minie's full, on-the-record commitment to the new dispensation. Accordingly, he prepared a Foreman's Newsletter for Minie's approval and subsequent dissemination to all supervisory personnel. The newsletter had an introduction that broached the news on the effort to bring the plant's equal opportunity policy to life (see Exhibit 9-1).

Minie went for it; the *Newsletter* appeared with the Introduction printed over his signature. Several days later, the third shift was eliminated, and the following week Kellogg began his human relations classes. They were given on the plant's premises, on company time, with the foremen attending in small groups.

The six workers rescued from the night shift were already on duty on the second shift when Kellogg held his first session. The nine foremen attending the class arrived in a belligerent mood, and Kellogg decided to let them air their questions first. He explained the human relations program almost the same way it had been described in the *Newsletter* and then called for discussion.

"Are we going to be held responsible for getting along with the black people who work here?" asked Tim Bronson. It sounded as if he were posing a question that the group had discussed earlier.

9-1. Introduction to Foreman's Newsletter.

As all our supervisors know, we have a written policy on equal opportunity and nondiscrimination in our plant. We are now starting a program that, we believe, will help us all to make this policy more effective. At the same time we believe our efforts in this direction will make our work relationships smoother, eliminate a lot of problems before they appear, and in general enable us to get on with our production jobs with a minimum of friction and time loss.

We are no different from other companies in doing what we are doing as regards these important policies. We are only interested in doing the job better. Nor are we asking that favoritism be shown any particular group of employees. That would be just as harmful as discrimination of a negative kind.

As a first step, we are starting, within the next month, a course in human relations for all supervisors. Class sessions will be scheduled in consultation with supervisory personnel. Our main objectives will include the following:

1. To discover ways in which supervisors can indicate, in speech and in action, that all employees, including our black employees, have each supervisor's respect, can trust supervisors to

9-1 (Cont.)

treat them fairly, and may count on supervisory help
in gaining the respect of fellow employees.

2. To enable supervisors to lead without using
pressure and to require the same level of job
performance from all employees so that all will gain
confidence in themselves and will have the
motivation to move ahead.

3. To find ways to deal patiently with short-
comings in any employees when these result from
honest misconceptions or from inexperience in an
industrial plant such as ours.

4. To explore ways to give constructive criticism
to all employees on the theory that such criticism
is essential to growth on the job and must be
accepted as constructively as it is offered.

5. To learn more about the need for supervisors
to recognize, both at first and later, that some of
our employees may require somewhat closer and
more explicit direction than others.

6. To learn to deal promptly, firmly, and fairly
with any display by any employee of animosity
toward any co-worker, and in this way to avoid
disruption on the job and violations of discipline
in our work groups.

7. To learn ways of handling matters of criticism
or discipline of black workers according to the

9-1 (Cont.)

principle, "What would I do if this were a white employee?"

8. To gain know-how in ways to enlist the aid of outstanding workers, black or white, so as to influence constructively any recalcitrant employee.

Miner B. Crane

Adapted from Paul H. Norgren, Albert N. Webster, Roger D. Borgeson, and Maud B. Patten, *Employing the Negro in American Industry: A Study of Management Practices*, Industrial Relations Monograph No. 17 (New York: Industrial Relations Counselors, Inc., 1959), p. 137.

"You're going to be held responsible for getting along with *all* your subordinates," Kellogg said. "You're also going to be held responsible for the working atmosphere of your areas. This is no different from what it has been. Now we're going to try to develop some techniques that should make it easier for all of you."

"But the company's trying to butter up the black employees, right?"

"Not at all." Kellogg felt himself bristling a little. He controlled himself carefully. "There are techniques to foremanship in a plant like this that we should all know. We are not asking for discrimination in reverse in any way, shape, or form."

"This *Newsletter*," said Tony d'Annunzio as he pulled a copy from his shirt pocket, "seemed pretty heavily oriented toward black workers. Are you telling us that this was a false impression?"

"Yes. I repeat: We want no discrimination in reverse. We *do* want you to remember that black workers may face certain problems that our white workers don't face."

"How do you handle a guy like Jones?" d'Annunzio shot back.

There it is, Kellogg thought. The trap. The question that had to be answered right or the word would be out among the foremen the moment the class was over.

"How do you handle Alton Carr or Mary Bianchi or Freddie Brown?" Kellogg asked.

"Tough," d'Annunzio smiled, looking around the group for approbation.

"Maybe that's something *you* should look at," Kellogg said quietly. The group's attention had begun to wander in response to d'Annunzio's comment; now it snapped back to Kellogg, who added: "If you're both tough *and* fair, you may be OK. But just remember: It's easier to go wrong, and make trouble in your department, if you're tough and even slightly *un*fair. Am I clear?"

"Clear," d'Annunzio muttered.

"Now can we get on with this?" Kellogg said. "We're trying to find ways to make a policy of nondiscrimination effective. We're trying to do it without showing favoritism to black workers. You've got to understand that warranted disciplinary action against any employee will be backed up, whatever the employee's color. You've also got to remember that you have the authority to criticize the work of any employee. Anything else would be unsatisfactory from everyone's point of view. But there are right and wrong ways to do all these things, and we have to find the right ways."

They were silent as Kellogg continued. When the class was over, they went back to work in a thoughtful mood.

He had a long way to go, Kellogg could see.

ESSENTIALS OF HARD-CORE COMMUNICATION

Kellogg was talking to Crane. "We're in hard-core hiring, but not yet in hard-core *employing*; That's the nub of it." Kellogg locked his hands behind his head, a typical gesture indicating he was thinking something through. "We're not in hard-core *communicating*—that might be a better way to express it."

"Well, you've got these classes going. They should help."

"They are scratching the surface. If you approve, I'd like to go a step further. We're getting across the theory—the business about understanding the ghetto experience, the lessons in the psychology of looking for work and raising a family when you're black and starting out, the techniques for giving orders, reprimanding, teaching new methods, and so on. But I've got to bring it down to the nitty-gritty."

"We've absorbed the classes, and from what I hear most of

the supervisors are accepting them. You've got my OK to go ahead."

"I don't know exactly what I'm going to go ahead *with*. But it'll be based on this thought: In an integrated workforce, communications *have* to have certain characteristics or they're doomed to fail." Kellogg took his hands down from his head. "I'll read you something. This sums up what I've got in mind as a target in the communications area."

Kellogg began to read (see Exhibit 9-2). When he was finished, Crane was studying him.

"What's your theory behind all this?" Crane asked.

"That there's bound to be some tension, at least under the surface, in an integrated situation such as we have. That if it's allowed to go unchecked, that tension can create major problems."

"Freeman Jones? The third shift?"

"That type of problem. Also the girls fighting at the time clock. Also problems like people walking off the job, such as happened in the assembly area the other day. This kind of thing is happening because we still have a way to go. And don't get me wrong, we'll never eliminate incidents and problems entirely. No company does. But we've got to take the initiative if we're even going to *minimize* the problems."

Crane was smiling. "You're educating *me* now. But why all the stress on our supervisors?"

"Because they're still the ones who can torpedo us. They may not be causing our problems except by omission. But the mistakes of omission are certainly there."

"OK. One more question: What if Tom and I and Jess act as the guinea pigs on some of the stuff you're proposing? The sensitivity training, for example?"

"You're on. I wish I had thought of that myself."

Kellogg left. Later, in his office, he had a visit from Freeman Jones. The man was smiling.

9-2. Characteristics of a communications system in an integrated workforce.

1. The entire communications system must be geared to the most basic common denominator, whether that denominator is the entry-level white or black worker. The communications system must also. . .
2. Be color-blind; it must draw no color lines whatsoever.
3. Be based on foreman-to-worker communication so as to achieve the most personal and universal kind of contact.
4. Utilize this key channel, foreman to worker, actually to overinform, in a sense, to provide more information than would in other plants and other situations be thought necessary.
5. Do this on the theory that overinforming is actually impossible in an integrated plant because the need for information is all-consuming.
6. Be built on listening, with instruction in listening included as a basic part of foremen's human relations training and with weekly foreman–work group information sessions required in every department.
7. Include, as part of the training in listening for foremen, some form of sensitivity training.
8. Deal not only with the staple materials for communication—production statistics, new products, capital expenditures, customers, product information, and so on—but, and just as important, with the why underlying the what—the reasons for change, adjustment, movement in one direction or another.
9. Utilize the normal modes of communication such as the plant newspaper and the bulletin boards, but do so with speed of delivery as a major goal.
10. Be launched by the General Manager so as to give the program all possible force of authority.
11. Be based in action, facts. Nothing speaks so loudly as what you do.

"Just thought you'd like to know," Jones said, "I got top production in our department for the second week in a row. Not bad?"

"Tremendous! That ought to make a believer out of d'Annunzio."

"I think it has. Anyway, things are really changing out on the floor there. I really think they're changing. Others have told me the same thing."

"Now you're telling me things I want to hear."

THE LONG CLIMB UPHILL

When something had gone downhill as long as human relations had in the Supreme Metal Stamping Company plant, it took twice as long to get them back up: That was the crux of it, in Kellogg's eyes. but he was launched, thanks to the backing of Minie Crane. The rest would be largely up to him.

He devoted long hours to it. He developed a policy manual for foremen that was to serve as a voice of authority on many of the things he was trying to accomplish, a voice that would speak at all hours of the working day to anyone referring to it—and always, it was to be hoped, in identical tones. Deep down, Kellogg knew that it was expecting too much to believe that every foreman would apply every policy in the same way in every case, but one could hope, couldn't one?

One of the first policy statements to go into the loose-leaf manual established the requirement that foremen were to meet with all their subordinates for 15 minutes each week (see Exhibit 9-3). If one group was too large, it could be divided into two groups, and the foreman would meet with each group separately. The foremen had the prerogative of choosing the days and times of meetings. They were, however, to follow a relatively patterned format for their meetings: Report to the group on matters that might be of interest to them and then

9-3. Foreman's meeting with employees.

It is established as plant policy that each regularly assigned foreman will hold group information meetings with subordinates on a weekly basis. Meetings will last for approximately fifteen minutes. Subordinate groups will attend the meetings in a body except where operational requirements make such a plan impossible, in which case the foreman will meet first with approximately one-half his work group and then, for an equal amount of time, with all remaining members of his group.

The purposes of the new information meeting program may be summarized briefly:

The meetings are intended, first, to give foremen an opportunity to become the first line of communication of company, division, department, or subdepartment informational material.

In the context of that effort, it is hoped that our workforce will become more knowledgeable about subjects of interest and concern to it. As experience has indicated, more efficient working relationships and more favorable work attitudes should develop as the program gains momentum.

Other objectives of the program include the following:

—Closer identification of the individual with the company through expanded knowledge and the development of an awareness of mutual interests;

—Encouragement of individuals to look beyond their own jobs;

—Encouragement of higher productivity, lower absenteeism and turnover, and better labor relations;

—Strengthening of the general role of the supervisor;

—Increased sensitivity on the part of supervisors to the problems of subordinates.

Plant management and the Personnel Department will cooperate in every possible way to make the information program function better, with success in the various goals as the target.

accept questions from meeting participants, with equal time devoted to each function.

Kellogg, passing through the plant after the policy had been in effect for a couple of weeks, noticed that John Teale was holding his meeting just before the lunch break. Kellogg went over to listen, and was surprised.

"We've explained all this meeting stuff to you before," John said, "but it might not hurt to go through it again for a second or two." He did, in very accurate terms, then made three or four announcements of departmental interest.

"That's about it," Kellogg heard Teale say. "Now we've got to have a few questions or Mr. Kellogg back there will have me strung up."

There was a nervous laugh. Then the questions started coming. They were good questions: "Can we expect more overtime now that those orders are starting to come in from Paxton?" "Can we have the area around the vending machines cleaned up more often?" "What's the company rule on wash-up time?"

Afterward, Kellogg was talking with Crane. "That one meeting went very well," Kellogg said. "I hope they all work out that way."

"Some will go well, some poorly," Crane said. "I think we have to expect that, at least until the foremen get the hang of this stuff. But maybe they're already getting the hang of it. What do you think? We seem to have a slightly different atmosphere around here."

"I'm hearing that," Kellogg said, "and I hope it's true. But I want to see it reflected in the P&L before I'll believe it."

"Meantime you're going to be cracking the whip over me."

"Got to. You can't stand still in this stuff or you go backward."

"So what's up your sleeve now?" Crane asked.

"You know that final line of my sketch of what a communications program should be in a plant like ours—the one that says your actions speak louder than anything you say?"

"Yeah?" Minie feigned nervousness.

"I know what we're going to do next: Name a black foreman."

Minie interrupted: "And we both know who it's going to be: Freeman Jones."

Kellogg was grinning. "You've got me wrong. The first black foreman in this plant will have to be selected on the recommendations of *all* the foremen, not just one, and on the basis of overall qualification. I think I'll go work out a policy on it."

10

When the Union Knocks

I'LL NEVER FORGET IT. As a personnel man, I had seen similar scenes, but this office vignette had a poignancy that the others lacked.

Charles Broadmain sat at his desk, uncharacteristically slumped, staring with blank eyes at his father's photo on the opposite wall. The only sound was a slight whisper as the small, black digital clock on the far side of the desk whirred to 4:33 P.M. From the wall Henry Broadmain, Charles's father and late president of Maintronics, Inc., seemed to stare down at the small brass plate on the clock's green onyx stand. *Charles Broadmain,* the plate read, *President and Chief Executive—In Honor of 25 Years of Service.*

Charles straightened up, hearing me at the door. His blue eyes flashed coldly. "Let me see it," he all but hissed. Silently, I handed him the crudely printed handbill.

As he read, my thoughts skimmed back quickly over the company's recent history. Nearly a year ago, a union had obtained 30 percent or more, probably many percentage points more, of our employees' signatures on election petitions and forced us into a representation election. As personnel director, I had managed the ensuing campaign with the help of a hastily recruited attorney who specialized in labor law. Of necessity, I had relied heavily on the attorney, who relied heavily on his law books. The whole sequence of events had been like a bad dream, but we had won the election by a narrow margin, favored, I believed, by the gods who watch over infants and fools.

The final vote, certified by the National Labor Relations Board, had given our company five more votes than the union. The certification had come after months of hearings and depositions, miles of testimony, and upswellings of bitterness that probably will never disappear completely.

Now the union was back.

"Why?" Charles asked. He had read the union handbill two or three times.

Charles was a curious admixture of old-fashioned paternalism and modern, technology-oriented, executive drive. He had remained eager to continue the growth pattern established by his father and grandfather for Maintronics; he nearly always, for example, approved justifiable new equipment and better methods of producing our specialty items—highly sophisticated electronics measuring equipment and parts for automated control systems. On the other hand, he ran our plant, located on the edge of a small southern town and employing 925 employees, in a blatantly paternalistic style. You could see it in the way he preferred the advice and counsel of his cousin, Peter Broadmain, executive vice president, and of his young nephew, Gardley Broadmain, who was in training for some as yet unspecified post. You could see it too in the way Charles addressed the plant's employees at the annual Christmas party.

His every tone in that canned annual speech said: "These are *my* people." The vote in the representation election gave back a different echo: 839 employees voted, giving the company a margin of victory slightly over 0.6 percent.

"Can you tell me what this is all about?" Charles asked me, nodding to indicate that I should sit down. "And where we go from here? We've been in business in this town for three generations. A lot of grandsons and granddaughters of our original employees are working here right now. Why has it all gone sour?"

ROOTS IN NEGLECT

A personnel man in a family-owned, paternalistic company has little power unless he belongs to "the family." I didn't. I was always allowed to speak my piece, but the big decisions, and most of the little ones, were made without great regard for my recommendations. This isn't bitterness; it's a simple fact.

The union men had appeared at our plant gate slightly over a year earlier. Carefully observing the rules about trespassing on company property, they passed out their handbills. I recommended a forceful campaign, but it never really got off the ground.

Well before that, I had heard talk that five or six employees were making strong medicine for a union. Foremen had reported that both men and women employees were asking pointed questions about pay and benefits, and about workplace conditions that never seemed to be taken care of. In some areas of the plant, people didn't seem as friendly as they had been; some even turned their backs when I came around. Little did they know how I had fought for changes, without success.

Ours was a closed company, if a healthy one in a business sense. Charles Broadmain made all the operating and personnel decisions. Everyone knew that. If he treated some workers better than others, if he gave some breaks or benefits or extra time off to some and not to all, what of it? We were all friends, weren't we? That was the attitude. Things would even out someday. I asked for policies to regulate those things and was called a crusader or, worse, a red-neck.

Another thing. At Maintronics, for the past 18 months

an affiliate of the conglomerate RJB Corporation, which never bothered us, communications was synonymous with Charles Broadmain. We had no handbook for employees, no policy manual, no company newspaper, bulletin, or news-sheet. Once in a while, Charles would put up an announcement on our solitary bulletin board. That always happened right after he and his cousin had decided on the pay raises and benefit improvements that would become effective three or four months later. Neither Charles nor his cousin ever talked to me about these changes. Most of the employees seemed to be satisfied, and that kind of boat is hard to rock.

"Why?" I said now, echoing Charles. "Because this is 1975, and workers everywhere are hungry for more of the good things. Also because we could do just a little more to keep these people on the company's side."

"Come on, Bryant—" Charles was going to say more, but his eye fell on the handbill. That changed his mind and mood; adversity is a sobering influence. "All right," he said, "what more could we do?"

"Get some real help in here before it's too late."

"What help?"

"That labor relations man who was here a couple of days talking to workers during last year's campaign. The one who's with RJB headquarters."

Charles was rubbing his chin. "Try it," he said. "What in hell can we lose?" As a second thought he added: "But what if he gives us another list of suggested changes?"

"This time I think we ought to follow through on them," I said.

WHEN TIME HAS RUN OUT

Both the lawyer and the labor relations man showed up in response to our calls. The lawyer was dogged in his pursuit of details that could hurt us legally. The labor relations man was shocked. "Time isn't short in this plant," he said, shaking his head. "It's run out. All we can do now is our best."

His name was Nolan Fairfax. He asked that our lawyer try in every possible way to buy time—delay an election. Then, in the presence of Charles and Peter and myself, he pulled a sheet of paper from his pocket. "This is the list of promises you made 11 months ago," he said. "Have any of these things been done?"

Charles scanned the list. I knew the answer, but I kept silent. "We gave the raise," Charles said.

"When?"

"Four months later, I guess—about July, Bryant?" He looked at me.

"August," I said. "It was actually due in May." I was rubbing it in.

"Well, that's water over the dam," Fairfax said. "What we've got to do now is look for a loophole in all this, a way we can reach the people. Then we'll need a theme for the campaign. In the meantime, we'll have to make some changes at the lowest level of operations."

He talked on. He wanted to meet with employees in small groups, and I had the task of setting up the sessions. On the basis of those meetings, he said, he would be better able to judge the temper of the plant. He also suggested that we prepare a letter to employees as soon as possible to warn them against signing union authorization cards. The letter would be sent if we could verify that the union was circulating the cards.

When the meeting broke up, everyone but Charles had something to do to get our counter-campaign under way. I had the feeling that things were moving at last, moving as they never could have moved without the impetus provided by the union organizers. In my office I said that to Fairfax, who had come with me.

"This is the tragedy," he said. "A basically well-intentioned management lets everything slide until it's under the gun of union organization, then it tries to repair all the damage in a matter of days or weeks. I think you and I can agree that unionization isn't the end of the world and that unions are necessary in some companies. But the truth is that they only get in where management creates the need for them."

"My sentiments exactly."

"What we've got to do now is get the communications ball rolling in two directions: one, to make management's feelings about the union clear, and two, to establish channels through which we can talk to people. We shouldn't have to do both of these things at once, but in this situation we have no choice."

THE COMMUNICATIONS BALL

Fairfax and I examined the alternatives, acting on the hopeful premise that we could probably talk Charles into anything at this point.

There was the matter of a theme for the counter-campaign. The year before, Charles had campaigned basically on the theme, "We're one big happy family and we don't need outsiders telling us how to run our business." The narrow election victory had exploded the happy-family bubble, and now, Fairfax and I agreed, we had to have another central idea or thesis for the coming few weeks. That theme would control what went into company communications regarding the union and, if scheduled, the election. The selection of theme could win or lose an election long before a single employee voted.

Just as important, we had to communicate with our employees. In most cases the methods of communication chosen would be new. Our existing programs were that primitive. We would want to communicate on subjects related to the union organizing campaign and on very many others unrelated to it. The methods we selected had to be effective and legal, as did the messages we would choose to deliver.

In the end Fairfax and I made a decision that, we believed, was dictated by reason as well as by circumstances: we would proceed along parallel paths of communication, using one set of means and techniques to deliver information related to the organizing campaign and another set of formats to deliver information not pertinent to the campaign.

We found out within two days that the union campaign was serious. Two employees came to my office with cards that the union organizers were passing out, signature cards of a standard type authorizing the union to act as a bargaining agent.

About the same time, we came up with a campaign theme that seemed the best available in the circumstances: "Give us a chance." The suggestion hidden in that theme was that family management had been so burdened by other responsibilities that it had not had time, really, to get its house in order. This was a patent misinterpretation but one that, we calculated, would at least awaken sympathy among many old-line employees.

The theme appeared in our first letter to employees' homes (see Exhibit 10-1), a relatively subdued document that was intended to demonstrate management's determination to keep its premises union-free. The letter also contained a warning to the effect that employees should be careful about signing union authorization cards. Written by Fairfax and myself and signed by Charles Broadmain after it had been checked by our lawyer, that first letter used simple language to convey its simple message to both employees and their families. We hoped it would slow down the union's effort

10-1. Letter to Maintronics employees' homes.

Dear Fellow Employee:

Look out! Once again the union is knocking on our door. This is the same union that tried to organize our plant last year. Obviously, it hasn't learned that you do not want to be unionized.

We are still convinced that we do not need a union in our plant. We can solve our own problems without the aid of a middle man at Maintronics—a middle man who really wants your dues. Do not be fooled by union promises! Or, better yet, when these union people start making promises, have them put it all in writing. See how fast they run.

Above all, be careful about signing union authorization cards. The cards could bring a union into our plant without an election. No one wants that—except the union itself. Then it could start collecting your dues without any more work. You would not even have had a chance to vote on union or no-union.

We want a chance to prove that we don't need a union here. We know you will give us that chance.

Sincerely,

Charles Broadmain

to collect signatures; with the names of 30 percent or more of our employees, the union could petition for an election— and get it.

We decided on other channels of communication on the organizing campaign: more letters, to be sent as the occasion seemed to warrant, a bulletin board for campaign material only, posters whose contents would be spelled out later, a get-out-and-vote contest, and so on.

In the meantime, for the first time, our plant began to see a concerted communications effort getting under way. For the first time, our employees began to learn in a systematic way what was going on in the Maintronics plant. Charles looked on these efforts with some disdain, but he went along with them. That in itself proved that he had been frightened by the latest organizing drive.

THE SMALL START

We started small. We distributed a one-page bulletin by means of "Take One" boxes located at strategic places throughout the plant. One box was located at each time-clock, for example. Others appeared, overnight, in our two vending areas and in the front offices, just outside my own cubbyhole.

We knew the danger in Take One boxes. Employees might scatter them around throughout the plant, leaving a colossal litter problem. We decided to take the risk. Essentially, we felt that our employees would respect their plant premises to the extent that they would not soil it with discarded paper.

I remembered what had happened outside our main employee parking lot the preceding year. Two union organizers had stood there passing out leaflets. Our people were streaming out, on foot and in cars. As they passed the organizers, leaflets were pressed on them. Few passed the organizers without taking one; few threw them down. An ominous sign, I thought then.

Now we were testing that principle in reverse. If our employees discarded management's news sheets in quantity, it probably could be read as a sign of generally unfavorable attitudes.

While the bulletins were in preparation, Fairfax and I spent a morning putting the newly launched communications program into perspective. Neither of us wanted to install a communications program that would be washed out when the union campaign ended, whether the campaign ended in victory or defeat for the company. But what to do?

"I'm for grabbing the initiative even if it means taking a chance," Fairfax said. I nodded agreement, and he continued: "We need contact with these people in addition to my meetings. Much of it will have to be face-to-face contact. We just don't have time to do it any other way."

"And face-to-face contact is more effective anyway."

"True."

We discussed other alternatives: areas where change might be introduced to build a case for concerned management. But in most such areas the risk appeared too great. We could not, for instance, make changes in wages and benefits without risking an unfair labor practice charge and perhaps losing the campaign. If a pattern of regular change had been established, that pattern could have been adhered to now, but of course no such pattern existed. We would face a similar problem if we attempted to install an effective seniority program. As regards supervision—

"We've got to meet with the supervisors," Fairfax said. "This has got to have priority, as you know."

I set the meeting for later that day. In the meantime I ran off some new copies of the basic guidelines to be used by foremen in communicating with subordinates during an organizing campaign (see Exhibit 10-2). We would give each foreman a copy at the meeting.

Before the foreman's meeting, Fairfax began his small group meetings with hourly employees. He kept these sessions to about half an hour, making notes as comments came from participants. I saw him after the first three meetings had already been completed, when the employees had returned to their work stations.

"What's the mood?" I asked, knowing full well from my own contacts in the plant what the answer would be.

"Bleak. Negative. But not hopeless at this point." He sat thinking. "From what a couple of people indicated—they didn't *say*, they only indicated—the union is getting dirty, and very serious."

"Like what?"

"They're starting to contact people at home. Some were called last night. Also, they're spreading lies about the company's profits over the past couple of years."

"It was bound to come."

"It came too fast. We're going to have to throw some fire back at them."

FIGHTING FIRE WITH FIRE

At the foreman's meeting, Fairfax and I made a big pitch for total cooperation to beat the union, collaborating in an effort to make it clear that much, and perhaps everything, depended on the foremen. They had it in their power to act as ambassadors for the company, to put its policies and actions in a good light. They could maintain an even tempo and a relaxed mood throughout the plant. If they chose, they could subtly influence individual allegiances—and votes. Equally important, they could act as our eyes and ears, bringing us information

10-2. Basic guidelines for union organizing campaign.

WHAT YOU, AS A FOREMAN, CAN SAY WHEN DISCUSSING
THE UNION ORGANIZING CAMPAIGN
WITH HOURLY EMPLOYEES

1. You can advise your subordinates about their rights under the law. Our employees are the only ones who may decide whether or not the union will represent them. But there is nothing in the law that requires an employee to vote for the union, even if he has signed a union authorization card.

2. You can inform employees that the election, if it comes, will be by secret ballot. Each employee may vote as he or she desires.

3. You can point out current wage rates and employee benefit programs that your subordinates presently enjoy without union membership.

4. You can advise employees that unionization may mean strikes, work stoppages, and picket lines, and you can cite the annual cost of union dues, special assessments, or initiation fees. Use caution here so as not to make the idea of a future strike appear to be inevitable.

5. You can question the union's claims, objectives, and assertions, provided that you do not threaten reprisal or promise benefits or advantages to discourage affiliation with the union.

6. You can argue that, in many cases, union policies and economic demands are set by union officials who do not work for the company and that these officials may have little knowledge of local plant or employment problems.

7. You can point out that it is the company and not the union that provides all wages and employee benefits and that union campaign promises of better wages and benefits, made now to the employees, are subject to collective bargaining and cannot be made

10-2 (Cont.)

good unless the company agrees to them. Be careful, again, not to threaten reprisal or promise benefits.

8. You can refer to any factual, truthful negative information about the union that has come to light as a result of investigation or publicity.

9. You can inform your subordinates about the significance of a union shop.

10. You can tell employees that their job security and the success of the business are not determined by the union but by customers who must be satisfied with the products we send them.

11. You can express the hope and belief that the employee will and should vote against the union, but it must be made clear at the same time that the employee has the final choice and the freedom to ballot as he sees fit.

12. You can point out that unionization means that a third party, the union, may come between the employee and the employer.

13. You can prohibit the distribution of handbills in work areas during both working and nonworking hours.

14. You can stop solicitation for union membership during working hours and in work areas only. This practice must be uniform in application to all kinds of solicitation, in line with general company practice.

15. You can refuse admittance of outside union organizers to the plant area or parking lot.

on what workers were talking about and were concerned with.

We had some explosive moments. Our foremen were conscientious; many of them had come out of the ranks of the workers, contrary to the practice in many plants in the South where class lines often inhibit upward mobility from line employee to lower management levels. A number of them felt strongly that our management had been extraordinarily dilatory about making needed changes. Their concern mirrored my own and Fairfax's, and we let them talk.

"Do you know we've had three skid loads of finished items overturn?" one foreman said. "That's because we can't get the flooring fixed in our department. It's not only dangerous—it's costing the company good money when we lose a skid."

"The women in my department have been bitching for months about the condition of their machines," said another foreman. "I think they're right, but we can't get the man we need to work on them. That's Joe Amberson, in maintenance."

A third noted: "My people are saying that the company will start moving on a lot of problems now that the union is back. I hope they're right."

Fairfax responded to that one: "From everything we've been able to learn, they are right. But we've got no choice. If they say that to your face, maybe you could let them know that this time it's going to take. There's a definite change of policy here."

I had time to ponder that response later. It meant, in essence, that Fairfax was keeping his superiors at RJB headquarters informed of progress in the plant and that they were probably not going to leave our family management to its own devices again after the election, whatever the outcome. In the meantime, the meeting went on and we had to field many more questions. When it was done, the foremen seemed relieved. I had made notes when they brought up workers' or their own suggestions for concrete changes. When they left, I reviewed the suggestions with Fairfax.

"Some of this repeats what I've been hearing from workers," Fairfax said. "It means we're really under the gun now. If we can't get action, and fast, we're wasting the listening."

"We'll get action," I said. I believed it.

Clearly, the battle was joined. Fairfax and I prepared a checklist of moves and strategies that we were launching or could launch in the future as the organizing drive unfolded (see Exhibit 10-3). The assumption underlying the entire list was that our listening efforts would bear fruit in terms of specific, concrete responses to workers' and foremen's ideas and suggestions. Such responses, given where justified, would complete the cycle of communication.

We had an answer the following day to the question whether Charles Broadmain would back us fully when we sought action from department managers, the maintenance people, and others. Fairfax and I were in Charles's office and had just started going down the list of suggested changes. Charles stopped us.

"I've appointed Jim Mulcahy to handle this stuff as it comes in," Charles said. "You can go straight to him. If he has any questions on the cost of any particular change, he'll come to me. But I don't think there will be any."

I could have sung out with glee. Mulcahy was the one man in our plant who could get *anything* done. He was a genuine miracle worker who often made a shoestring do the work of a ship's cable: one of those people who believe that half the battle in an industrial plant is removing obstacles to an employee's desire to do good work.

I went to Mulcahy. He *had* been notified that he was to assume the job of troubleshooter, action manager, instrument of change, or as he good-naturedly expressed it, "gripe co-

10-3. Checklist of possible management moves.

—Establish "listening posts" throughout the plant, using both foremen and reliable employees.

—Communicate as fully and freely as possible on all subjects of interest to employees while the organizing drive is under way.

—Enforce the no-solicitation rule continuously and unexceptionally.

—Review and update, and use where necessary, material employed in earlier organizing campaigns.

—Review the plant's supervisory force, looking for weak or inconsistent foremen.

—Line up community sources of information.

—Make sure the personnel department reviews all disciplinary actions.

—Make certain the personnel office serves as a communications center for all campaign information.

—Know your opponent; have some research done on the union that is seeking to organize the plant. Also check on its officers.

—Know the internal organizers; watch maintenance and inspection in particular since personnel in these sections have broad access to many plant areas.

—Know, or find out, the union's strike history, constitution and bylaws, financial position, and so on.

—Prepare a chronological listing of company wage and benefit improvements.

—Study the background of NLRB decisions for the plant's specific area.

—Make certain that there are no outstanding, legitimate complaints or grievances.

—Anticipate employee reactions to any actions undertaken by management during the campaign.

—Prepare the "Personal Strike-Loss Computer" and a fact sheet on the union, as well as other documents and speeches as soon as they appear to be appropriate additions to the counter-campaign.

ordinator." There was no need to go down the list point by point with Mulcahy; he simply ran his eye down it and said: "We can take care of this stuff in 24 hours, Bryant, if you want."

"I want," I said. "I think we should do it as unobtrusively as possible, Jim." He nodded.

We were in business. Our listening-plus-action campaign meant that we were really fighting the union's fire with some powerful flames of our own. Now we had some hope that we hadn't started too late.

END ON A "NO" VOTE

The rest of that campaign became a blur of activity that kept me awake many nights.

Within a couple of weeks the union had petitioned for, and had been granted, an election. The date was set about six weeks ahead.

Fairfax and I worked 12 hours a day. He stood totally aside from the nitty-gritty of the campaign, concentrating rather on the physical changes that were being made in rapid-fire order by Jim Mulcahy and a crew from Maintenance, continuing his listening, working with the foremen both individually and in groups.

Sometimes we thought our own people were working against us. A department manager, one from the old authoritarian school, demanded that his foremen confiscate and burn any union literature that they saw or found, even if they found it on a worker's person. He also suggested that his supervisors work their people so hard that "they won't have time to think about a union." That set our clock back somewhat in that department, but we caught the problem in time to set both the record and the party line straight with both department manager and foremen.

In one case we turned adversity to our own advantage. A foreman, noting that a male employee was wearing a VOTE UNION button, went up to the man, tore the button free, and then threw it down and stepped on it. Within 24 hours we had moved the foreman, a notoriously non-simpatico type, to a job involving no direct supervisory functions. Almost at once the mood in the foreman's old area improved measurably.

Our two-pronged communications campaign moved ahead steadily. The bulletin boards we had set up to promulgate information on the campaign rapidly filled up as we added posters and memoranda. Some of this material was "straight," and included simple announcements such as one regarding the date of the election and the rules governing it. Other material had to rank as propaganda. For example, one item listed "Ten Questions You Can Ask the Union Organizers and Sympathizers" (Exhibit 10-4). In the meantime, our communications efforts regarding the company, its employees, and its products were answering questions that had interested or bothered our people for years. We had indications that many employees welcomed it.

In the background, day by day, we had that unceasing voice behind us: that of the union. *"More money, more benefits, more security, more voice in company matters, more cash for overtime, more compulsory job classifications, more guarantees—This is what you will get with a union,"* one handbill screamed. Another: *"By going to an election, the company is gaining precious time and will save thousands of dollars by holding off the date when increased wages and benefits will be put into effect under your union contract."* Still another: *"Can you imagine that your reward for a lifetime of service to this company could be a pink slip for not getting the high production rates the company has set?"* As I mused on what effect that last would have on our employees, especially our older employees who would know

10-4. Campaign propaganda.

TEN QUESTIONS YOU CAN ASK THE UNION ORGANIZERS AND SYMPATHIZERS

1. Can you [the organizers or sympathizers] guarantee that the union will deliver on its campaign promises in the event that the union should win the election?
2. Will you put your promises in writing?
3. Is it true that unions, once in a plant, fight overtime for employees of that plant so that the company will have to hire more workers, who will pay the unions more dues?
4. Is it true that unions—
   (a) May bring strikes, violence, picketing, and the like?
   (b) Sometimes levy fines, special assessments, and other charges on members in addition to initiation fees, dues, and so on?
   (c) Insist on superseniority for all stewards, officers, and officials in the plants where they work?
5. Do members of a plant organizing committee usually become the shop committee in the event the union wins the election?
6. Do union officials' and agents' salaries go on while a strike is in progress?
7. Is it true that the only thing a union can really promise in an organizing campaign is that the union will negotiate with the employer if the union wins the election?
8. Is it true that not all employees of a company may vote on whether to strike or not—but only those who belong to the union and are dues-paying members in good standing?
9. Is it true that where such union members vote to strike, all employees of the firm, whether union members or not, are usually forced to stop work?
10. Is it true that only about 25 percent of American workers belong to labor unions?

that Maintronics invariably kept people on beyond retirement age and much later if they could work, I read another paragraph:

"Isn't it strange how much faster the company's heart beats for you at union time? Actually it's all a coverup. They know unions mean improvements in wages and benefits— an end to 'security through favoritism' and the bosses' 'promote the pets' plan. Beware of love letters to your home with juicy tidbits about one big, happy family!"

Actually, we were avoiding the "big happy family" theme like the plague.

As we came down to the election wire, I drafted a "twenty-four hour" speech that Charles would deliver. It had to be given no less than 24 hours before the day of the election. With 925 employees working three shifts, we had to devise a schedule of meetings as intricate as the schedule of a major airline. At the end of the day Charles was so hoarse he could hardly talk.

On the day of the election, I stayed in my office. In one way I was sorry it was all over but the balloting. It had been an exciting time. We had fought a good fight; win or lose, we had nothing to be ashamed of.

I stood at the window. I could look down across the parking lot. There the union organizers stood, again passing out handbills. Fairfax came in as I watched, staring down through thin rain at the figures beyond the parking lot entrance. A very few people were entering the plant on foot or in cars.

"Lot of wet handbills down there," Fairfax said at my elbow.

He was right. A lot of employees were simply dropping the union handouts at the organizers' feet. Another cleanup job for Mulcahy, I thought. Then the significance of what I was seeing came to me.

"It's a good omen," I said.

Early the next morning, when the votes had been counted, we had proof that I had been right. The company won the election by 24 votes, a slightly larger margin than the preceding year.

Charles had gone to his club to await word on the results. As I dialed his number, seeing before me in the next office the two National Labor Relations Board officials who had supervised the balloting, I had the sensation that I was living this scene for the last time, that now we could settle down and really make a happy family of this workforce. Our people had given us another chance.

Epilogue

TEN CASES, TEN SOLUTIONS. Ten different approaches? Not quite. Each approach has a thread of commonality: Each includes a readiness to provide the psychological room in which the employee-objects of the motivational efforts could grow.

Each involves listening, the "open mind" characteristic that gives meaning to individual managerial styles geared to what has been termed the motivation crisis of the 1970s.

The crisis has been described. It subsists under diverse names and appears in widely disparate circumstances—sometimes, as in the ten cases, in relatively extreme forms. Its causes have been outlined: a "failure of communications" has occurred, or a morale problem (dubious term) has arisen because a manager has committed the error of assuming a God-given right to control others. A problem may eventually appear susceptible of cure only if participative management methods can be introduced and made effective, with a more transactional management attitude as the keystone. The cases considered here suggest that the crisis need not be perpetuated.

In one instance, a manager facing an embittered union averted disaster in the productivity sphere by introducing a full-scale listening program, *cum* consultant, and superinducing a "Hawthorne effect." As the latter developed, the workforce came to feel management's intense interest in the workers' needs, desires, and welfare and gradually put its collective shoulder to the productivity wheel.

In the second case, a plant manager working with a college-trained foreman in a key production area encouraged—and taught—the foreman to overcome his youth and lack of production experience. The foreman listened, took the mental pulse of old-timers in his department, and eventually took the initiative in establishing a new working relationship, in the process overcoming intense personality resistance.

A third case portrayed a real-life "listening" manager as he eliminated, stage by difficult stage, a departmentwide production limitation. The method: to work initially at removal of demotivators—negative "hygiene" factors—and then to reinforce the existing motivators.

In situation four, the women's liberation movement came to life in a plastics plant, producing a tone of deep dissatisfaction among the Extrusion department's female employees and posing a threat against the higher-paid male employees. Listening within and outside the plant, involving assessment of government guidelines on equality of the sexes, produced a solution that met the needs of both sides, established equality, and changed the basic distribution of skills and wages very little.

The fifth case turned on the absolute need to obtain creative approaches to problems through use of the new tools of the 1970s: altered states of consciousness. In a plant without obvious problems, a company president changed forever a complacent, don't-rock-the-boat attitude among his managers by introducing them to confrontation sessions.

In the next situation, policy in a white collar organization had taken precedence over humaneness to the point where four key employees resigned at once. A personnel man restored balance as he was forced to listen, alter his stance, open his mind, and in the end launch a unitwide communications/motivation program keyed to employees' specific interests and needs.

In the seventh case, a plant in a deteriorating urban environment faced the need to relocate to the suburbs to avoid possible production and productivity losses expected as skilled middle-class employees became harder to find. A determined plant manager with an ability to listen worked with a consultant as he launched an aggressive community relations campaign in the neighborhood and in the process won the loyalty and cooperation of *all* employees.

A research facility, in the eighth case, failed signally to obtain the necessary cooperation of its creative personnel, the research chemists, because it had adhered to authoritarian, line-management concepts. The facility's manager listened, installed a less rigid system geared to the facts of the creative research situation, and ended by establishing a climate that produced a remarkably high-performance group.

The ninth case dealt with a highly sensitive situation evolving during a plant's transition from an all-white to a black-and-white employee force. A personnel man ascertained the facts during a series of listening efforts, then took full responsibility for a genuine integration program in *employment* as well as in *hiring*. A communications/motivation effort sprang to life along guidelines specifically devised to meet the challenge of integration.

In the final case, a union was making its second try to organize a southern plant's workforce. The stresses and strains developing in such a situation were handled by a "listening" personnel man and a professional "listening" consultant; a new, broadly based communications effort functioning in two separate arenas, the campaign itself and the general area of communication, took shape with such good effect that the company won the election and earned an opportunity to put its communications/motivation house in order on a long-term basis.

What are the implications of all this? They are society-wide. "The less effectively organizations carry out the work of society, the greater the cost in money and social paralysis," as Levinson notes.* This remains true even though the crisis of today has evolved partly as an afterburn of industrial success. Once again, we come face to face with the basic human needs hierarchy. "We can produce success with KITA's," Herzberg comments, "but once people have success they no longer are moved by KITA's."† They become interested in the wider issues of life: They even begin". . . to ask the question consciously and in ever increasing numbers, 'How do we spend our lives . . . ?'"‡

In macrocosm as in microcosm. The motivation crisis is amenable to listening-based therapy within the small circle of the plant or shop; it must, therefore, also be treatable in the larger circle of society. This poses very directly the ultimate challenge for the manager. If, as he has done in these ten cases, he can solve major internal communications/ motivation problems, has he not also made an approach to solution of a wider societal problem—of alienation, of anomie, of loss of identity, of inequality, of prejudice, of call-it-what-you-will?

Nothing could have more pertinence for business and industry today, or for all of society tomorrow.

---

*Harry Levinson, "Asinine Attitudes Toward Motivation," *Harvard Business Review,* January-February 1973, p. 71.

†"An Interview with Frederick Herzberg: Managers or Animal Trainers?" *Management Review,* July 1971, p. 14.

‡Ibid., pp. 14, 15.